GW00584780

THIS THING WE CALL LITERATURE

Une discussion littéraire à la deuxième Galerie

THIS THING WE CALL LITERATURE

ARTHUR KRYSTAL

OXFORD
UNIVERSITY PRESS

OXFORD

UNIVERSITY PRESS

Oxford University Press is a department of the University of Oxford. It furthers
the University's objective of excellence in research, scholarship, and education
by publishing worldwide. Oxford is a registered trade mark of Oxford University
Press in the UK and in certain other countries.

Published in the United States of America by Oxford University Press
198 Madison Avenue, New York, NY 10016, United States of America

Library of Congress Cataloging-in-Publication Data
Names: Krystal, Arthur.
Title: This thing we call literature / Arthur Krystal.
Description: New York, NY : Oxford University Press, 2016.
Identifiers: LCCN 2015042157 | ISBN 9780190272371 (hardback) |
ISBN 9780190272395 (epub)
Subjects: LCSH: Literature, Modern—20th century—History and criticism. |
Literature and society. | BISAC: LITERARY COLLECTIONS / Essays.
Classification: LCC PN771 .K75 2016 | DDC 809—dc23 LC record available at
http://lccn.loc.gov/2015042157

1 3 5 7 9 8 6 4 2

Printed in the United States of America
on acid-free paper
Printed by Sheridan, USA

CONTENTS

ACKNOWLEDGMENTS

My thanks to Henry Finder at the *New Yorker*, Deirdre Foley-Mendelssohn at *Harper's*, and Evan Goldstein and Alexander Kafka at *The Chronicle of Higher Education*. A special note of appreciation goes to the indefatigable fact checkers at these magazines who on more than one occasion saved me from embarrassment.

I am also grateful to Suzanne Ryan and Joellyn Ausanka of Oxford University Press, who steered the book through the choppy waters of publication.

AUTHOR'S NOTE

Looking over the present collection, I see that I have restated certain opinions (hitting the same nail with differently weighted hammers) and sometimes resorted to the same references. There's something lazy about this, and I apologize to those readers who choose to read the essays in sequence. But there is also something right about judicious repetition. Like a certain Mr. Hazlitt, I am glad to see that "if I have felt any impression once, I feel it more strongly a second time; and I have no wish to revile and discard my best thoughts."

Some years ago a reviewer saw fit to note the frequency with which Hazlitt pops up in my essays. For this I make no apologies; Hazlitt remains an essayist whom every writer should read. He doesn't appear in these pages at all. Instead, it's Lionel Trilling who hovers over or even permeates the book, which makes sense given that many of these essays address the meaning and evolution of literature. Trilling was possessed by literature. In essay after essay, he seems to be asking: "What is it that literature depends on for its effect?"*

---

* This formulation appears in my essay "Club Work," which documents the coming and going of the Readers' Subscription Book Club, later renamed the Mid-Century Book Club, whose editorial board consisted of Trilling, Jacques Barzun, and W. H. Auden.

His answer was as inconvenient and dichotomous as one might expect. In characteristic dialectical fashion, he described literature's power stemming from both "the aesthetic effect of intellectual cogency" and something *primitive* "which is of the highest value to the literary artist."

However literature was viewed in Trilling's day, and it certainly wasn't as a monolithic entity, there was little ambiguity about what people meant by it. It's only in the past thirty years or so that literature has come in for a battering or, more charitably, a makeover. Figuratively, physically, and geographically, it has a new look. Internet books and Internet opinions festoon the virtual globe, and books themselves are more international than ever before. As to literature's intrinsic or unquestioned qualities, it's safe to say only that mainstream novels, once considered peripheral to serious study, have in many colleges become the mainstay of literature. Indeed, popularity—the "pop" in Pop Culture—has for all intents and purposes lost its paradoxically outlier connotation. Whereas Popular Culture studies once conveyed a whiff of nose-thumbing at the establishment or at least constituted a more fun aspect of English studies, its syllabi are now as blandly received as any list of "Great Books."

Is this necessarily bad? That depends on your expectations. If you think that *Buffy the Vampire Slayer* deserves to be the subject of an academic dissertation in English or that the Tarzan books belong in the literary canon because they have been anointed by the Library of America, then you are living at the right time. Elitist literary culture is as defunct as Buffalo Bill, a semi-elitist reference that thirty or forty years ago would have been familiar to serious readers. Apart from such high-minded and right-of-center periodicals as *Commentary* and the *New Criterion*, where are Maya Angelou, Stephen King, and Nora Roberts taken to task for the quality of their minds or the vigor of their sentences?

Given our anti-elitist culture, distrust of the canon, and deference to the public's literary taste, we tend to honor those books whose sales suggest that they are revealing something important about ourselves. One could argue, as Karl Kraus did, that minor or popular writers tell us more about a nation's state of mind than works of genius do—but is that the purpose of literature? On the one hand, writers ought to make us aware of how people live and what they're thinking and feeling. On the other hand, literature is an art and not meant to be convenient: significant poems and novels are created not for the casual reader but for those who appreciate how writers accommodate and deviate from each other's work. This doesn't automatically exclude the less sophisticated, but it might, and so be it.

Although writers shouldn't be punished for their popularity—Dickens, as anti-elitists never tire of pointing out, was very popular—they also shouldn't be exalted for it. There's nothing wrong with admiring Elmore Leonard without likening him to Proust or Henry James. Leonard has his skills *and* his place in literature without exactly being part of literature as Trilling understood it. Trilling wrote at a time when the modernist novel and poem were deeply honored, when T. S. Eliot and Yevgeny Yevtushenko drew enthusiastic crowds to their readings. Hardly anyone thought it necessary to redefine literature. What mattered was not whether a book sold well but that a small but vocal minority felt that it deserved their attention. Yes, I mean those dreaded urbanized intellectuals who lived and breathed books and saw fit to pronounce judgment for the rest of us. Whatever compulsions drove them, whatever ambitions summoned their efforts or evasions, whatever debts or grievances needed to be discharged, they judged books not out of hubris or because they wished to hold the fort against the less privileged, but because they were besotted by books, because the ecstasy they felt when reading great verse or prose was the reason—well, one of the reasons—for being alive.

If the literary world was once smaller and not as tolerant, it was less from some ideological program than from a protectiveness for a dream, for the idyllic notion that perfection might be glimpsed. But to live for literature was decidedly not a dream; it was an unwavering constraint, as though temperament or genetic disposition consigned certain people to a fate of forced, hapless, and passionate reading. And because of this predilection, literature hooked them, and when pure it both enslaved and enthralled them.

Fifty years ago we opened books not just to learn about the content of a writer's mind but to hear the right words in the right order telling us things we sensed to be true. Books got us high because they entered our bloodstream. To read Donne, Herrick, Keats, Yeats, Dylan Thomas, Fitzgerald, Proust, James, and Joyce was like hearing Miles or Louis on the horn or Art Tatum or Bill Evans on the keyboard. By God, back then we *listened* when we read, and if on occasion our ears needed readjustment, we read the same words again and again until we heard what we were supposed to hear.

Do people still feel that way? Do we still have a touching faith in the idea that literature gives life meaning? I may be traveling in the wrong circles, but I can't help thinking that the romance of books is swiftly disappearing. There's too much clamor, too much noise about the books that will scarcely matter to future generations. Everyone reads, everyone has an opinion, and those opinions fly at us from every corner of the Internet. There used to be something special about books precisely because literature existed as a category that brooked no dissent. Literature was as real as the person who experienced it, and in some sense it lay waiting for us, waiting to be triggered by something we read at twelve or fourteen. We were taught to read but not to love reading; *that* came unbidden. "You cannot teach someone to love great poetry if they come to you without such love," Harold Bloom noted. "How can you teach solitude?"

So it comes down, as it must, to one reader reading, one person who understands that he or she, while alone, is still part of a select society, a gallery of like-minded readers who, though they may disagree about this or that book, know that literature matters in a way that life matters. Such readers, I believe, still exist. I wish them well. I wish them literature. And I wish them solitude.

THIS THING WE CALL LITERATURE

1

WHAT IS LITERATURE?

There's a new definition of literature in town. It has been slouching toward us for some time now, but may have arrived officially in 2009 with the publication of Greil Marcus and Werner Sollors's *A New Literary History of America*. Alongside essays on Twain, Fitzgerald, Frost, and Henry James, there are pieces about Jackson Pollock, Chuck Berry, the telephone, the Winchester rifle, and Linda Lovelace. Apparently, "literary means not only what is written but what is voiced, what is expressed, what is invented, in whatever form"—in which case, maps, sermons, comic strips, cartoons, speeches, photographs, movies, war memorials, and music all huddle beneath the literary umbrella.

Books continue to matter, of course, but not in the way that earlier generations took for granted. In 2004 "the most influential cultural figure now alive," according to *Newsweek*, wasn't a novelist or historian; it was Robert Zimmerman, aka Bob Dylan. Not incidentally, the index to *A New Literary History* contains more references to Dylan than to both Stephen Crane and Hart Crane. Dylan may have described himself as "a song-and-dance-man," but Marcus and Sollors and such critics as Christopher Ricks beg to differ. Dylan, they contend, is one of the greatest poets this nation has ever produced (in point of fact, he has been nominated for a Nobel Prize in Literature every year since 1996).

The idea that literature contains multitudes is not new. For the greater part of its history, *lit(t)eratura*, from the Latin *littera* (letter), referred to any writing formed with letters and pertained to all written materials. Until the eighteenth century, literature, as Raymond Williams pointed out, was "a category of use and condition rather than of production." The only true makers of creative work were poets, and what they aspired to was not literature but poesy. A piece of writing was "literary" only if enough Learned Readers spoke well of it; but as Thomas Rhymer observed in 1674, "till of late years England was as free from Criticks, as it is from Wolves."

So when did literature in the modern sense begin? According to Trevor Ross's *The Making of the English Literary Canon*, that would have been on February 22, 1774. Ross is citing with theatrical flair the case of *Donaldson v. Becket*, which did away with the notion of "perpetual copyright" and, as one contemporary onlooker put it, allowed "the Works of *Shakespeare*, of *Addison*, *Pope*, *Swift*, *Gay*, and many other excellent Authors of the present Century ... to be the Property of any Person." It was at this point, Ross claims, that "the canon became a set of commodities to be consumed; it became literature rather than poetry."

What Ross and other historians of literature credibly maintain is that the literary canon was largely an Augustan invention, evolving from *la querelle des Anciens et des Modernes*, which pitted cutting-edge seventeenth-century authors against the Greek and Latin poets. And because a canon of vastly superior ancient writers already existed—Homer, Virgil, Cicero,

Seneca et al.—a modern canon had been slow to develop. One way around this obstacle was to create new ancients closer to one's own time, which is precisely what John Dryden did in 1700, when he translated *The Canterbury Tales* into Modern English. Dryden not only made Chaucer's work a classic; he helped canonize English literature itself.

The word *canon*, from the Greek, originally meant "measuring stick" or "rule" and was used by the Church Fathers to differentiate the genuine or canonical books of the Bible from the apocryphal ones. Canonization, of course, also referred to the Catholic practice of designating the saints, but the term was not applied to secular writings until 1768, when the German classicist David Ruhnken spoke of *canones* of ancient orators and poets. The usage may have been novel, but the idea of a literary canon was already in the air. As early as 1593, a Cambridge don suggested that universities "take the course to canonize [their] owne writers, that not every bold ballader...may pass current with a Poet's name." And Descartes, in 1637, opined that "the reading of all good books is indeed like a conversation with the noblest men of past centuries who were the authors of them, nay a carefully studied conversation, in which they reveal to us none but the best of their thoughts."

A similar nod toward hierarchies appeared in Daniel Defoe's *A Vindication of the Press* (1718) and Joseph Spence's plan for a dictionary of British poets. Writing in 1730, Spence suggested that the "known marks for ye different *magnitudes* of the *Stars*" could be used to establish poetic rankings such as "great Genius & fine writer...fine writer...middling poet...one never to be read." Twenty-five years later, Joseph Warton's "An Essay on the Genius and Writings of Pope" designated "four different classes and degrees" of poets, with Spenser, Shakespeare, and Milton comfortably leading the field. Finally, Samuel Johnson's *Lives of the English Poets* (1779–1781) confirmed the canon's constituents—fifty-two of them—and also fine-tuned standards of literary merit, so that the common reader, "uncorrupted with literary prejudices," would know what to look for.

In effect, the canon formalized modern literature as a select body of imaginative writings that could stand up to the Greek and Latin texts. Although exclusionary by nature, it was originally intended to impart a sense of unity; critics hoped that a tradition of great writers would help create a national literature. What was the apotheosis of Shakespeare and Milton if not an attempt to show the world that England and not France, especially not France, had produced such geniuses? The canon anointed the worthy and, by implication, the unworthy, functioning as a set of commandments that saved people the trouble of deciding what to read.

The canon—later the canon of Great Books—endured without real opposition for nearly two centuries before antinomian forces decided enough was enough. I refer, of course, to that mixed bag of politicized professors and theory-happy revisionists—feminists, ethnicists, Marxists, semioticians, deconstructionists, new historicists, and cultural materialists of the 1970s and '80s—all of whom took exception to the canon while not necessarily seeing eye to eye about much else. Essentially, the postmodernists were against—well, essentialism. While books were conceived in private, they reflected the ideological makeup of their host culture; and the criticism that gave them aesthetic legitimacy served only to justify the prevailing social order. The implication could not be plainer: if books simply reinforced the cultural values that helped shape them, then any old book or any new book was worthy of consideration. Literature with a capital L was nothing more than a bossy construct, and the canon, instead of being genuine and beneficial, was unreal and oppressive.

Traditionalists, naturally, were aghast. The canon, they argued, represented the best that had been thought and said, and its contents were an expression of the human condition: the joy of love, the sorrow of death, the pain of duty, the horror of war, and the recognition of self and soul. Some writers conveyed this with linguistic brio, others through a sensitive and nuanced portrayal of experience; and their books were part of an ongoing conversation, whose changing sum was nothing less than the history of ideas. To mess with the canon was to mess with civilization itself.

Although it's pretty to think that great books arise because great writers are driven to write exactly what they want to write, canon formation was, in truth, a result of the middle class's desire to see its own values reflected in art. As such, the canon was tied to the advance of literacy, the surging book trade, the growing appeal of novels, the spread of coffee shops and clubs, the rise of reviews and magazines, the creation of private circulating libraries, the popularity of serialization and three-decker novels, and, finally, the eventual takeover of literature by institutions of higher learning.

These historical trends have all been amply documented by a clutch of scholarly works issuing from the canon wars of the 1970s and '80s; and few critics today would ever think to ignore the cultural complicity inherent in canon formation.[1] Consider, for example, the familiar poetry anthology. As

Barbara Benedict explains in *Making the Modern Reader*, the first anthologies were pieced together less out of aesthetic conviction than out of the desire of printers and booksellers to promote books whose copyrights they held. And because poets wanted to see their work anthologized, they began writing shorter poems to increase their chances for inclusion.

By the early 1800s, according to Thomas Bonnell, author of *That Most Disreputable Trade*, uniform sets of poetry or the "Complete Works" of writers were standard publishing fare; and because the books looked and felt good—*The Aldine Edition of British Poets* (1830–1852) was bound in blue morocco and marbled boards with gilt on the front covers and spines— each decorative volume seemed to shout "Literature." But it was literature with a small paradox at its center. Because each set was "complete" (though volumes might be added later), a uniform edition was a hierarchy without levels. Wordsworth, for one, resented John Bell's edition of *The Poets of Great Britain* (1778) because Abraham Cowley and Thomas Gray held the same pride of place, simply by inclusion, as Chaucer and Shakespeare.

But it would be small-minded, as well as excessive, to claim that commerce alone drove the literary enterprise. The fact that writers and publishers had *gelt* as well as gilt on their minds does not diminish the role of individual genius in the creation of canonical texts. Simply because serialization influenced the composition and length of novels doesn't mean that writers tossed aesthetic considerations aside.[2] Canon formation continued to rely on a credible, if not monolithic, consensus among informed readers.

In time, the canon, formerly the province of reviews and magazines, which disseminated the opinions of Johnson,

Coleridge, Hazlitt, and Arnold, was annexed by institutions of higher learning, which cultivated eminent professors of English and comparative literature—Erich Auerbach, F. R. Leavis, Northrop Fry, et al.—and later recruited famous poets and writers to act as gatekeepers, shoring up the classics while keeping out the riffraff. Books now became our cultural capital, an investment one made in the hopes of acquiring knowledge and character. In 1909 Charles W. Eliot, the president of Harvard, claimed that anyone could earn a sound liberal arts education simply by spending fifteen minutes a day reading books that fit on a "five-foot shelf."

The shelf, as it turned out, held exactly fifty-one books, which were published by P. F. Collier & Son's as *The Harvard Classics* and went on to sell some 350,000 sets. Eliot's exhortations notwithstanding, the books were a publishing rather than an educational venture. It wasn't until John Erskine of Columbia and Robert Maynard Hutchins of the University of Chicago lobbied, in the 1920s, for a list of indispensable works in literature and philosophy that the canon became equated with a syllabus.

More than anyone else, however, it was Erskine's student Mortimer J. Adler who popularized the idea of the Great Books. Adler, who also ended up at Chicago, went on to write the bestselling *How To Read A Book* (1940), whose appendix of "Recommended Reading" (all of it "over most people's heads") served as a springboard for the 1952 *Encyclopaedia Britannica's* ancillary fifty-four-volume series Great Books of the Western World, selected by—who else?—Adler and Hutchins.

Although the canon could groan and shift in its place, as late as 1970 there was probably little disagreement as to what constituted literature.[3] Despite the Nobel Prize being awarded to some unlikely recipients, as well as to Bertrand Russell, literature generally meant the *best* literature; and the canon, despite the complicity of institutions and the interests of those involved in the promotion of books, was essentially an aesthetic organism, tended by literary and academic gardeners.

In a sense, the canon was like an imposing, upstanding tree, an elm or Sierra redwood, whose main branches originally consisted of epic poetry, comedy and tragedy, a few satires, some religious and philosophical treatises, and the shorter poems and prose works of various Greek and Roman writers. As the tree aged, other limbs formed that were capable of supporting Elizabethan drama, nineteenth-century novels, and collections of essays, short stories, and lyric poems. Adler's list of Great Books enumerates 137 authors, representing about four times as many books, including works by Newton, Poincaré, and Einstein. Adler, who died in 2001 at the age of ninety-eight, may have regretted his strong constitution. The tree he had helped cultivate now bent dangerously beneath the weight of its own foliage. Other genres— mysteries, thrillers, science fiction, fantasy, and horror— extended from the trunk, sprouting titles that Adler must have bristled at, including those by women and minority writers whose books flourished, so it was claimed, because of their sex and ethnicity.

In the late 1970s, the anti-canonites began taking over the universities; and the English-department syllabus, the canon by another name, was dismantled. It wasn't only postmodernists who lowered the boom. Even critics who wrote for general-interest magazines appeared to be fed up with the idea that some books were better for you than others. Leslie Fiedler, for one, owned up to his susceptibility to not-so-great novels in *What Was Literature?* (1982). Fiedler maintained that he had been brainwashed by highbrow criticism to the detriment of his own natural enjoyment of pure storytelling. Certain novels, despite "their executive ineptitude and imprecision of language," moved him, and he wasn't going to deny it. Such novels, he argued, appealed on some primitive level of storytelling; they expressed our need for myth and archetype and had to be considered literature even "at their egregious worst."

Fiedler wasn't going against the grain. By the end of the last century, a reaction against the high modernism of Eliot and Pound had set in. Ambiguity, complexity (obscurity), wit, and lyricism—the traits that Hutchins and Adler thought indispensable to literature—had lost their appeal. And no writer was immune. In 1989, Gary Taylor's popular *Reinventing Shakespeare* concluded that the Bard "was no less and no more singular than anyone else." Taylor's final sentence was a clarion call to every reader put off by Joyce or Proust: "Sycophancy in the arts is no more admirable in literature than in politics." Which, of course, is what Marcus and Sollors's *A New Literary History of America* is also quietly advocating. Despite the editors' protestations that their goal "is not to smash a canon or create a new one," it's hard to view their kaleidoscopic idea of "American speech" as anything but a means to demystify and downgrade the singularly verbal quality of the literary work.

Terry Eagleton has recently gone one better, questioning whether "something called literature actually exists." In *The Event of Literature* (2012), Eagleton, who once proposed replacing departments of literature with "discourse studies," refuses, thirty years after the publication of his highly readable *Literary Theory*, to cede to literature a single objective reality. As he did in his earlier book, Eagleton incisively surveys the theories addressing literature and concludes that it can't really sustain an overarching definition, since there is nothing verbally peculiar to a literary work, and no single feature or set of features is shared by literary theory.

In sum, we live in a time when inequality in the arts is seen as a relativistic crock, when the distinction between popular culture and high culture is said to be either dictatorial or arbitrary. Yet lodged in that accusatory word "inequality" is an idea we refuse to abandon. I mean, of course, quality. The canon may be gone, but the idea of the canon persists.[4] Penguin Books is now issuing a series of "modern classics," which the publisher has decided are classics in the making. No doubt some of these novels deserve our consideration— Evan S. Connell's *Mrs. Bridge* shouldn't offend even unrepentant highbrows—but what about those books shoehorned in because they occasioned "great movies" or constitute "pure classic escapism"? Do Charles Williford's *Miami Blues* and Nick Hornby's *Fever Pitch*, enjoyable as they are, rate as modern classics? Clearly, the idea of greatness continues to appeal, and just as clearly our definition of it has changed—as has our definition of literature.

Eighty-five years ago, in *The Whirligig of Taste*, the British writer E. E. Kellett disabused absolutists of the notion that books are read the same way by successive generations. Kellett concluded his short but far-ranging survey by noting that "almost all critical judgment ... is in the main built on prejudice." This, of course, makes consensus about books only slightly more probable than time travel. But if there is even a remote chance of its happening, the first thing we have to do is acknowledge our own deep-seated preferences. The adept critic Desmond MacCarthy once observed that

> one cannot get away from one's temperament any more than one can jump away from one's shadow, but one can discount the emphasis which it produces. I snub my own temperament when I think it is not leading me straight to the spot where a general panorama of an author's work is visible.

Although the snubbing of one's temperament is not easily accomplished, we can try. We can move from being ecstatic readers to critical readers, hesitating to defend a book because we like it or condemn it because we don't. For when it comes to books, it isn't always wise to follow our bliss when bliss gets in the way of reason, and reason alone should be sufficient to tell us that *War and Peace* is objectively greater than *The War of the Worlds*, no matter which one we prefer to reread.

Here's the trick, if that's the right word: one may regard the canon as a convenient fiction, shaped in part by the material conditions under which writing is produced and consumed, while simultaneously recognizing the validity of hierarchical thinking and aesthetic criteria. Writers may not be able to "escape from contingency," as the New Historicists used to say, but those sensitive to their respective prisons *can* transform the walls that confine them—a transformation that requires an awareness of the great poets and novelists who preceded them. Influence can be both confining and freeing.

So whether one gives the nod to Walter Jackson Bate's aesthetically modulated historical burden or to Harold Bloom's idea of largely unconscious misreadings, artists look backward in order to move forward. Which is why hierarchical rankings of writers are as natural as those teeming lists of great boxers, tenors, composers, and cabinet makers. The canon may be unfair and its proponents self-serving, but the fact that there is no set-in-stone syllabus or sacred inventory of Great Books does not mean there are no great books. This is something that seems to have gotten lost in the canon brawl—i.e., the distinction between a *list* of Great Books and the *idea* that some books are far better than others.

In a word, Marcus and Sollors are wrong. "Literary" does not refer to "what is expressed, what is invented, in whatever form," and literature does not encompass every book that comes down the pike, however smart or well-made. At the risk of waxing metaphysical, one might argue that literature, like any artifact, has both a Platonic form and an Aristotelian concreteness. Although examples of imaginative writing arrive in all sizes and degrees of proficiency, literature with a capital L, even as its meaning swims in and out of focus, is absolutist in the sense that all serious writers aspire to it. Writers may be good or bad, but literature itself is *always* good, if not necessarily perfect. Bad literature is, in effect, a contradiction. One can have *flawed* literature, but not bad literature; one can have something "like literature" or even "literature on a humble but not ignoble level," as Wilson characterized the *Sherlock Holmes* stories, but one can't have dumb or mediocre literature.

The truth is, we want from poetry and prose what Bob Dylan and even many well-written commercial novels cannot provide. (Unnecessary disclosure: I began listening to Dylan in 1965 and have never stopped.) We want important writing (bearing in mind that not every successful poem or story need be utterly serious) to explore the human condition, and we want our writers to function, as Eliot said of the metaphysical poets, as "curious explorers of the soul." Such exploration may be mediated by personal as well as historical forces, but the work will always reveal nature to be more obdurate than the institutions that seek to channel it. Indelible truths, as Auden might say, stare from every human face, and they are not at the whim of regime change. So while lesser writers may summon enthusiasm or indifference, great writers power their way into our consciousness almost against our will.

More than the distinctive knit of his prose, a writer is what he (or she) chooses to write about, and his commitment to tradition is what enables his work to spring free. Put another way: the canon is the meeting place where strong writers, in Harold Bloom's agonistic scenario, strive to outmuscle their precursors in order to express their own individuality. That's what literature is—isn't it?—a record of one human being's sojourn on earth, proffered in verse or prose that artfully weaves together a knowledge of the past with a heightened awareness of the present in ever new *verbal* configurations. The rest isn't silence, but it isn't literature either.

2

PRÉLUDE

Of Resistance and Celebration

Paris. February 26, 1635. The Abbé François de Boisrobert stands before the newly minted Académie Française and denounces Homer as a base street poet who eked out a living by declaiming his verses to the mob. Boisrobert's impassioned speech was perhaps the first skirmish in *la querelle des Anciens et des Modernes*, whereby one group of writers sought to position itself at the expense of those who continued to venerate the Greek and Latin poets. It was the seventeenth century, the Renaissance was winding down, Copernicus and Kepler had changed the cosmological map, William Harvey's anatomical study *De Motu Cordis* had dispatched the humoral theory, and poets, whose charge was to instruct as well as delight, had to make sense of a world "all in pieces, all coherence gone, / All just supply, and all Relation."

But the ancients couldn't be dislodged so easily. When the corpus of Western literature consisted largely of two dozen writers who had set the standard for plays, essays, verse, and satires, it was no simple matter to consign them to the past, especially when the past was still present. The historical sense, as we know it, was not yet fully developed. Herodotus and Thucydides, to be sure, had written histories, but the idea of the past as an area of fruitful study by which modern men could improve upon the work of their predecessors was by no means the received wisdom. As Steven Shapin put it in his capably succinct *The Scientific Revolution*, "the idea of linear, cumulative intellectual progress was still novel and not widely accepted."

But once scientists and philosophers began to question accepted models of the cosmos, relying more and more on empirical observation—urged on by such works as Francis Bacon's *The Advancement of Learning* (1605) and Robert Boyle's *The Sceptical Chymist* (1661)—progress in the arts became a reality as well. Indeed, it was rather daring of Bacon to flout convention by scolding authority for denying "time his rights, who is the author of authors, nay, rather of all authority. For rightly is truth called the daughter of time, not of authority." In short, people of a later age must know more than those who had come before.

This may not strike us as a startling proposition unless we recall that for almost two millennia there was nothing new under a sun that revolved around the earth. Most people in Western Europe believed that Jesus had put the world on a schedule that would end with His coming (more imminent than distant), an expectation that did not offer much incentive to challenge long-held assumptions.[1] Ironically, it was the Renaissance's esteem of ancient texts that led to the scholarship that gradually found chinks in those texts and the commentaries based on them. As Joseph M. Levine noted in his wholly admirable *The Battle of the Books*, humanist scholars "began to perceive anomalies in the old authors, and something of their strangeness—and to set them at a distance." By developing philological techniques of evaluation and interpretation in order to test what the ancients knew, humanist scholars created a fissure "between imitation and scholarship, rhetoric and philology, literature and history."

It was one thing, however, to attempt an understanding of ancient texts from the standpoint of the people who wrote them and quite another to grasp the idea that they could be surpassed. Even Bacon was reluctant to dismiss the ancients out of hand. If the moderns saw further, it was because they were able to stand on the shoulders of the giants who had come before.[2] The point was not so much to denigrate ancient wisdom and art as to put them in perspective and encourage modern writers to strive for a similar excellence. Too much veneration for Homer, Pindar, and the Greek playwrights, for Seneca, Cicero, Virgil, and Ovid would only compel modern poets to imitate them.

Although Boisrobert's opinions were heresy to many, they were undoubtedly heroic to those writers who thought the ancients needed to be updated. Surely, they could not have said everything there was to say. What did the ancients know of firearms, printing, or the nautical compass? Montaigne, who died in 1592, wouldn't have thought a choice between ancients and moderns was even necessary. Nor, if I can speculate broadly, did the fact of poets and essayists arguing their own cause sustain the quarrel. Rabelais (1494–1553), Cervantes (1547–1616), and Shakespeare (1564–1616) certainly created works never seen before; nonetheless, even they were not sufficient for the moderns to prevail.

It wasn't just the anxiety of influence or the idea of progress that drove our first moderns; it was something less tangible, a discernible shift in expectations, in the way that writers regarded themselves. Perhaps Donne's *First Anniversary* (1621) managed to identify it. The *Anniversary* wasn't only about the loss of "commerce twixt heaven and earth"; it was also about the rise of subjectivity, the belief that each human being imagines himself unique:

> For every man alone thinks he hath got
> To be a phoenix, and that then can be
> None of that kind, of which he is, but he.

And if you're a phoenix and a poet too boot, just how much obeisance is due the ancients? Had they, in truth, achieved perfection—in which case, imitation was the only recourse—or could a modern-day writer express himself in ways the ancients could never have envisioned? Although most writers were not inclined to dispute Aristotle's *Poetics* or Horace's *Technique of Poetry*, they *could* question whether the unities of time and space, which limited the action, or the rules of decorum, which dictated subject matter, had to be observed so rigorously.

As literary quarrels go, this was a particularly good one. *La querelle des Anciens et des Modernes* wasn't really about writing but about the quality of ideas, about the relationship between knowledge and innovation, and not least about the value of originality. Before the eighteenth century no self-respecting writer (who, after all, had been weaned on the ancients) would have wanted to divorce himself from the very authors who had formed his education. The past wasn't something to surpass or circumvent, but to adapt and make relevant. On the other hand, once the present began to seem divorced from the past, modern writers felt they knew more than had their ancestors, and in order to distinguish themselves from both the ancients and their own contemporaries, they had to write works unbeholden to previous efforts. In Edward Young's *Conjectures on Original Composition* (1759), we find the notion that "the first ancients had no merit in being originals; they could not be imitators. Modern writers have a choice to make and therefore have a merit in their power."[3]

I allot so much time to this old dispute because in one form or another it has never gone away. From the Elizabethans to the Augustans and on through the romantics, Victorians, and modernists, writers have grappled with precursors and established standards. But it is only recently that the "Battle of the Books" has assumed a different cast entirely. Toward the end of the last century, a loose confederation of critics and philosophers decreed that modernism consisted of work that was too oblique and too self-consciously "high art" while remaining at the same time innocent of its own socio-semiotic implications.

But what made the postmodern charter different was its willingness to discard the very idea of standards. Starting from the premise that aesthetics were just another social construct rather than a product of universal principles, postmodernist thinkers argued that all forms of writing—from broadsheets to billboards—possessed existential significance. One could learn as much about human experience from "Peanuts" as from *Buddenbrooks*. Such theorists were not only provocative; they were also persuasive. By uncovering the socioeconomic considerations behind canon formation, they had many readers wondering if they hadn't been bamboozled by Arnoldian acolytes and eloquent ideologues.

That heretofore inviolable ideal of art, as expostulated by Walter Pater and John Ruskin, by T. S. Eliot and Lionel Trilling, by the New Criticism, was shunted aside; and those emblematic qualities of modernist works—obliqueness, lyricism, dissonance, ambiguity—were relegated to a hubristic past. Although many former canonical authors continue to be taught in universities, they now share space with popular, commercial, and genre writers. As long as a writer is able to accumulate sufficient readers and a decent press, surely respect must follow. Any reason that George R. R. Martin shouldn't have parity with William Faulkner? Should Maya Angelou be less important than Emily Dickinson?

These are curious times for those who regard books with strict discernment. According to science-fiction writer Ursula K. Le Guin, "Literature is the extant body of written art. All novels belong to it." Le Guin's defiantly ecumenical statement is aimed at anyone professing to see a distinction between genre fiction and literary fiction, which, according to Le Guin, is an illegitimate demarcation that falsely demeans good genre writing and excuses bad literary writing.[4]

There is certainly nothing wrong in holding genre to the same standards as any other kind of writing, but there is also no reason to hold it to less rigorous standards. While the beginning to *The Big Sleep* is aces in my book, it still isn't serious literature, for the simple reason that Chandler didn't intend it to be. It's perfectly fine to like Chandler—you'd have to be a real sourpuss not to—but that doesn't elevate his fiction to major literary status. The difficulty, of course, lies in distinguishing one kind of appreciation from another. Who's to say that one poem, play, or novel is better more or meaningful than another?

It would be nice to report that people of similar temperaments and backgrounds immediately discern which books qualify as art and which don't, but that just isn't the case. In fact, the entire question of what is and isn't literature resembles a televised debate between presidential candidates followed by the predictable reactions of registered voters, each side convinced that its own candidate won. The critic and novelist Lev Grossman looks at the opening to Agatha Christie's *Murder on the Orient Express* and thinks it "masterly"; I glance at it and see only competence. Who's right?

There's no getting around the problem of taste, because any solution is also a matter of taste. My own taste inches toward Hume's idea of disinterested pleasure. It may seem willfully anachronistic to rely on an eighteenth-century theory of perception, but I don't know a better way of forming aesthetic judgments. Hume thinks we should familiarize ourselves with what gives us pleasure until we're able to view that object (and others like it) with a detachment arising from a greater understanding of how the object's purpose and construction fit together. Essentially, Hume is advising us to move from being ecstatic readers to being informed readers. He's telling us to tamp down our biases and preferences and to rely on experience tempered by learning.

Good luck! But just because it's difficult to know which books stand above the rest doesn't mean we should give up. Edmund Burke, according to Macaulay, "generally chose his side like a fanatic, and defended it like a philosopher." In the case of the literary canon, may I suggest that we embrace it like a philosopher and defend it like a fanatic?

Nonetheless, I'm not so foolish as to believe that I started out philosophically. When I was growing up, no one told me that *The Three Musketeers* or the Sherlock Holmes stories were tales I should read; they were simply books that, once picked up, I *had* to finish. But when Stendhal and Dostoevsky and Gogol first fell into my hands, I became alerted to the fact that I was *supposed* to read, that reading was something I was good at. Although I didn't know there was a canon, I knew that some authors were manifestly more intelligent, more thoughtful, more skilled than others. How could they not be?

While there is nothing wrong (and perhaps even something right) in praising those whom previously we shunned, a law of diminishing returns kicks in once we stop making distinctions between the great and the good. It's one thing to acknowledge the socioeconomic factors of canon-building and another to remove the aesthetic scaffolding of works that reflect time, skill, effort, and intelligence. What ardent defenders of merely good or commercial books find hard to credit is that those of us who stand by the canon (lacunae and all) feel just as ardently. It's just that our feelings are secured by the apprehension that some books reflect a deeper understanding of the world, of history, of human relationships, of literature itself than do other books. One can certainly like James Crumley and James Lee Burke, and one can rave about Robert Heinlein, Phillip K. Dick, J. K. Rowling, Orson Scott Card, or any number of good genre writers, but one can't *love* them in the way that one loves Shakespeare, Keats, Henry James, and James Joyce. One can be a fan of Agatha Christie, but one can't really be a *fan* of George Eliot.

"The history of literature," Lionel Trilling remarked, "is never quiet for long and is never merely an additive kind of growth."

Speaking very generally, as fiction gradually replaced poetry as our primary reading matter, additive growth took the form of mimetic representations of reality. Whether presented in the gritty language of Raymond Carver or the verbal swoops and whooshes of David Foster Wallace, fiction summons a world that is both recognizable and relevant. Fabulistic or familiar, it probes the human condition to reveal the implications of class, race, sex, love, alienation, and the conflict between individual and communal values. And to bring this off, authors rely more on accuracy of characterization than on the events that their characters react to. It's what separates great novels from merely good or pleasurable ones. It's the difference between *Anna Karenina* and *Bridget Jones*.

Although intelligent, well-informed readers can both overpraise and undervalue specific novels, their idiosyncratic readings do not disprove the fact of definable gradations in intelligence or skill. Nabokov, for one, disliked both Dostoevsky and Faulkner, not to mention Mann, Malraux, and Bellow. Nonetheless, he would have flicked his butterfly net at a former president of the Modern Language Association who declared that choosing between Virginia Woolf and Pearl Buck is "no different from choosing between a hoagy and a pizza." Idiosyncrasies have their place, and we ought to make allowances for them. But what are we do with William James's admission that "[a]s a rule reading fiction is as hard to me as trying to hit a target by hurling feathers at it. I need *resistance* to celebrate!"?

It's a tough audience that dismisses Sterne, Balzac, Stendhal, Hawthorne, and James's own brother. Still, we know what James meant. There's not much at stake in a novel by Nora Roberts or Clive Cussler. The reason people enjoy these books is the same reason that other people cannot celebrate them:

they don't make us *think*. I can only speak for the person who brushes my teeth, but what I want from literature, at least some of the time, is what Trilling christened "the aesthetic effect of intellectual cogency": passages of verse and prose whose combinations of thought and language, of form and content, are so seamlessly integrated that the pleasure one derives from understanding the text is almost physiological in nature.

Which doesn't mean that I can't savor or esteem what William James found less than challenging. If I may indulge in a bit of chest-thumping, I was reading Elmore Leonard in the mid-1970s, long before he was a household name and years before Martin Amis and other literati discovered him. This doesn't make me especially percipient; Leonard could write, and I liked reading his novels (his Westerns, too). Nor did I feel particularly guilty about setting aside *The Ambassadors* to romp through Frank Herbert's *Dune* trilogy. To state the obvious: There's a place for P. G. Wodehouse and James Thurber, for Eric Ambler and Ross Thomas, for any number of thriller and adventure writers. There are times when only *The Long Goodbye* will do or Stephen Becker's *Chinese Bandit* or____(you fill in the blank).

But let's not make more of these books than we should. The fact is, most writers don't aspire to the type of intellectual cogency that impressed Trilling, nor should they; and unless sluggishly inept or gloriously inane, their books don't trouble us. But for a variety of reasons our cultural arbiters have decided to level the playing field. The prevailing mood (I hesitate to call it the conventional wisdom) regards hierarchies with suspicion: Who's to say who is worth reading and who isn't? The liberal allocation of excellence, a byproduct of the culture wars of the 1970s and '80s, is an old story by now, exemplified by the self-esteem movement in public schools and the demotic willingness to include formerly disenfranchised artists and writers. This isn't necessarily a bad thing; sometimes it's proper to reevaluate a writer who has been ignored or dismissed.

That said, the fact that writers are all entitled to a fair hearing doesn't mean that they are equal. It doesn't require much effort to recognize that the vast majority of popular novels (the Kings, Steels, Cartlands, Pattersons, et al.) do not provide what serious literature offers. Does this mean that every literary novelist is wonderful in all respects? Not at all. There are plenty of serious writers whose sentences and pacing could use a bit of work. Dostoevsky wasn't exactly known for his *mots justes*, and Dreiser could have profited from lessons in elementary exposition. But say what you want about *Ulysses*—and many readers have said that it's boring and impossible to read—it's hard to understand how anyone sensitive to language could fail to be impressed by Joyce's facility with it.

Toward the middle of the last century, Erich Auerbach went to great lengths to show that the nature of writing changes along with the nature of the reading public. By examining the grammatical and stylistic tropes that writers inherit from their predecessors, as well as the innovations they hit upon, Auerbach demonstrated that writing dramatically changed between the early Middle Ages (when there was no literary public) and the second part of the seventeenth century (when such a public appeared in France). For Auerbach, the circumstances surrounding the creation of specific works and the relationships between them at the time of their conception, and the ways they become viewed by subsequent generations, was "an endless problem which each of us, exerting the utmost concentration, must endeavor to solve for himself and from his own point of view." In other words, judgment should be deferred until one appreciates the stylistic singularity of texts and the historical circumstances of their genesis.

What Auerbach is telling us—what every good critic implicitly asserts—is that a serious evaluation of books relies on something other than the private experience of reading. Although literature begins with pleasure, the requirements of pleasure become more complicated as we gradually demand from books something more than a juicy story, though plot should never be discounted. As William Godwin observed in 1797, "the impression we derive from a book, depends much less upon its real contents, than upon the temper of mind and preparation with which we read it." True insofar as it goes, but what Godwin neglects to say is that the contents—that is, the very books we choose—follow from our "temper of mind and preparation" and, in fact, help constitute them. To some degree, we are what we read, and what we read has a bearing upon what and how we read in the future.

None of which matters when it comes to convincing people that one opinion is better than another. Likes and dislikes cannot be argued away, especially if one comes to books without a proper education in books. It may seem perfectly natural to me to differentiate between the great and not-so-great-books, but that doesn't mean I can persuade others which books belong to the canon and which don't, or that a canon is the natural outcome of writers wishing to differentiate themselves from each other. What I can state is that while the democratization of literature serves a purpose, it is not necessarily for the betterment of literature.

There are consequences of removing the canon, or, perhaps more accurately, an absence of consequences. Without a canon of Great Books, Donne's phoenix is free to rise unfettered by pieties and paradigms. Without a canon, every autodidact with a bad teacher can have his or her day in the digital sun. Without a canon, literary authority in the guise of a critic, magazine, or institution is dissipated. Now add to the mix an Internet where every book, every critical evaluation, is almost immediately swept aside by another—what is left to hold onto?

As I look around, it seems to me that we live amid a great sprawl of what passes for literature; and though one can sympathize with readers who don't like being told what to read, there is simply too much chatter out there to know which books merit further study and which don't. Which leads me to wonder if all this doesn't affect the way that poets and novelists write.

The first generation of writers who saw themselves as a distinct communal entity had to account for the Greek and Latin masters who had died nearly two millennia earlier. By maintaining that their works rivaled in significance, if not in skill, that of the ancients, they started the ball rolling and, in effect, laid the foundations for the canon. Unless I am mistaken, the last generation to take real issue with their precursors appeared during the culture wars of the 1970s and '80s, when the distinction between high and low collapsed and the literary canon disappeared in a puff of self-righteous, egalitarian smoke. As I look around today I can't help wondering if the ball hasn't finally come to a stop. Whom do our poets and novelists seek to supplant, and what aesthetic or philosophical precepts ride on the attempt?

Although serious writers continue to work in the hope that time will forgive them for writing well, the prevailing mood welcomes fiction and poetry of every stripe, as long as the reading public champions it. And this, I think, is a huge mistake. Literature has never just been about the public (even when the public has embraced such canonical authors as Hugo, Dickens, and Tolstoy). Literature has always been a conversation among writers who borrow, build upon, and deviate from each other's words. Forgetting this, we forget that aesthetics is not a social invention, that democracy is not an aesthetic category, and that the dismantling of hierarchies is tantamount to an erasure of history.

3

SHOULD WRITERS REPLY TO REVIEWERS?

Fifteen years ago, I made a decision to stop reviewing books. I stopped because my inner *préfet* was always looking for an excuse to emerge. Given a book to review, I'd snap on my pince-nez, straighten my waistcoat, and get down to business. I was worse than officious: I was clever. If a sentence lost its way, if a character stepped out of line, if a fact failed to meet its obligation, I would, with a buttery phrase or sly allusion, put the author on notice. I was fair, of course (what reviewer *isn't* fair?), but I can't say that I minded scoring points off another writer's mistakes.

Here's the not-so-hidden secret of book reviewing: many writers, especially younger ones, regard other people's books as an opportunity to enhance their own reputations. What better way to show off one's own wit, erudition, and verbal artistry than to debunk someone else's? And if you can look good at some poor writer's expense—well, why not? Edmund Wilson, himself a formidable reviewer, lamented that reading reviews of his own books, "whether favorable or unfavorable, is one of the most disappointing experiences in life"; and the novelist Arnold Bennett claimed he never read his reviews, he only measured them. "Reviewing is not really a respectable occupation," W. H. Auden alleged. "A reviewer is responsible for any harm he does, and he can do quite a lot."

You bet he (or she) can. A few catty, well-placed reviews can kill a book faster than a burning pyre. Those of us who watched Dale Peck beat up on Rick Moody's *The Black Veil* in the *New Republic* and David Gates tear into Tim O'Brien's *July, July* in the *New York Times Book Review* felt a little scorched ourselves. But for pure malicious bloodletting nothing beat Joe Queenan's *New York Times* review of A. J. Jacobs's *The Know-It-All*. Although I happen to think Queenan was right, his review was so gratuitously nasty that one couldn't help thinking that the editor of the *Book Review* knew it would cause a ruckus, which it did, even prompting an entertaining rebuttal from Jacobs entitled "I Am Not a Jackass."

No writer, however ignorant or inept, should be placed in this position. Queenan overstepped not by finding fault but by deliberately taking center stage. He didn't review Jacobs's book so much as punish the man for having written it. A far less harsh review would have served just as well, since most authors are never satisfied with a review unless it's a flat-out, without-reservation rave. Imagine, then, what an ambivalent or disparaging report does.

Kingsley Amis, in a moment of weakness, allowed that a bad review could spoil a writer's breakfast, but not his lunch. Really? Recipients of unfavorable reviews suffer heartburn for months, perhaps years. And why shouldn't they? Reading a stupid review is a little like being mugged. You feel violated and outraged and want nothing less than to see the perp caught and publicly flogged. But what can you do? Everyone knows that disgruntled authors are advised to keep quiet, since any rejoinder can only make them look peevish while at the same time calling even *more* attention to a harsh critique.

No, there isn't much an author can do except console himself with the fact that a great many literary works have been poorly received. One of the most famous examples is Keats's *Endymion*, savaged in print by men whose names signaled their affectionate natures. In 1818, a certain John Lockhart sneered at "the calm, settled, imperturbable drivelling idiocy" of Keats's poem in *Blackwood's Magazine*, and a month later the Tory writer John Croker cruelly mocked the author in the *Quarterly Review*: "We...honestly confess that we have not read his work. Not that we have been wanting in our duty...indeed, we have made efforts almost as superhuman as the story itself appears to be." Croker then asked those who *could* finish it to write to him. Although Keats lived to compose another day (not many, to be sure), Byron, who was even less fond of reviewers than of Keats, decided that the poet "was killed off by one critique, / Just as he really promised something great.... 'Tis strange the mind, that very fiery particle, / Should let itself be snuffed out by an article."

The practice of book reviewing regularly comes in for its share of judicious or sanctimonious scrutiny. Goethe bemoaned the quality of book reviewers in the early nineteenth century, and Elizabeth Hardwick did the same in 1959, claiming that "sweet, bland commendations fall everywhere upon the scene; a universal, if somewhat lobotomized, accommodation reigns." Hardwick faulted the book-review sections of *Time*, the *New York Times*, and the *Herald Tribune* for their middlebrow blather and urged them to seek out "the unusual, the difficult, the lengthy, the intransigent, and above all, the *interesting*."

More recently, a serious albeit somewhat woolly essay by Elizabeth Gumport appeared in *n+1*, condemning the entire enterprise of journalistic reviewing. Tom Lutz followed up with a sensible monograph in the *Los Angeles Review of Books* that accepted both the necessity and built-in fallacies of the review process. However one chooses to regard them, book reviews perform, if nothing else, a public service, a service that is now also performed by the public. I allude, of course, to the Internet with its myriad of reviewer-bloggers whose opinions rain down like confetti on Amazon and other websites devoted to books.

Whatever one thinks of all these "nonprofessional" reviews, it's bracing, I suppose, that so many people feel compelled to weigh in. I say "nonprofessional" not because such opinions arrive unbidden, but because they make no bones about being anything but highly personal responses. Indeed, whatever their merits, they demonstrate that *all* reviews—professional or otherwise—are personal. Here I part company with Daniel Mendelsohn, who, on accepting the NBCC's 2001 Nona Balakian Citation for Excellence in Reviewing, observed that reviewing "isn't a personal thing between the critic and the author." Well, no, not from the standpoint of wanting to please or displease a stranger who happened to write a book, but one can't simply ignore the fact that *someone* put in the time and effort to research, document, imagine, edit, and revise. This doesn't give authors a free pass, but let's be honest: an offense against a book is an offense against the person who wrote it.

And while we're on the subject, let's put to rest another misconception: a bad review is not—I repeat, is not—better than no review at all. Where does such homiletic bunk come from? Yes, it's better to be indifferently noticed than completely neglected, but no writer enjoys a review that lords it over his or her book. And while a bad review will sell more books than no review at all, it will not sell many and certainly not enough to compensate the author for seeing his or her work publicly slighted or, worse, mangled.

It may not surprise you to learn that reviews of my own books have not always gone down well. My work has been both warmly and lukewarmly received, which does not mean that the favorable reviews were any more accurate than the mildly disparaging ones. In one case, a reviewer who liked my last collection of essays stated that I had saved the best essay for last. Not true. So why should the nineteen people who actually pick up my books anticipate that after the sixth essay a better one lies in store? Another reviewer, meanwhile, a British novelist, seemed put out that, unlike Christopher Hitchens, I never asked the US Special Forces to waterboard me in order to write an essay about it. I am ashamed to say that I did not remedy this situation for the present collection.

I'm not complaining—OK, I am complaining, not because reviewers find fault but because, given a chance to perform, they forget they're rendering a service to the reader, not one to themselves. A flawed book gives no one license to flog it in print. If there are mistakes, why not sound regretful when pointing them out instead of smug? If the book doesn't measure up to expectations, why not consider the author's own expectations with regard to it? While no one wants shoddy work to escape detection, a critic must persuade not only the impartial reader but also the biased author—as well as his biased editor and biased family—that the response is just.

And tone is crucial, tone is all. Even reviewers who check their personalities at the door often condescend without meaning to. Perhaps it can't be helped. There's a reason, after all, that a judge's bench overlooks the courtroom: sentences must appear as if passed down from on high. I'm not saying only Buddhists should review, but wouldn't it be nice if the superior attitude, the knowing asides, and the unshakeable convictions could disappear from the world of print? From personal experience, I can tell you that my own books have been discussed by people who had no idea what most of my essays were about, but whose pontifical airs demonstrated (as if further proof were needed!) that lack of knowledge is never an obstacle to self-esteem.

Am I suggesting that book reviews are necessary evils? Not at all. A smart, well-written critique is always a welcome guidepost in this torrential age of virtual and print publishing. Plenty of fluent literary evaluations sound just the right note of judicial appraisal and collegial appreciation. It's only those reviews *with attitude* that stick in my craw and make me wince at the thought of the ones I used to write myself. And perhaps because I've worked both sides of the street, I now presume to speak for authors who feel they've been maligned or misrepresented. My advice is: Get mad and stay mad. Don't cry, don't pout, don't feel helpless. Just because there's nothing you can do doesn't mean you should do nothing.

In effect, I'm taking back what I said earlier. What the hell, make noise! Call attention to the offending review. In fact, write that letter to the editor that everyone enjoins you not to write, and in a few deft strokes outline the reviewer's bias and how he or she misread, obfuscated, and distorted your work. Then write another letter, this one to the $#%^ reviewer, and explain exactly where he or she went wrong. Address the reviewer's objections intelligently and dispassionately. You don't want to sound like Alain de Botton, who informed a critic, "You have now killed my book in the United States.... I will hate you till the day I die and wish you nothing but ill will in every career move you make"—but it wouldn't hurt to sound slightly unhinged, just to make the perp wary of running into you at a party or book signing. Maybe if more reviewers felt they were dealing with a human being and not a bound galley, their own words might be a bit less brazen, a touch less supercilious next time out.

4

EASY WRITERS

Guilty Pleasures without the Guilt

W hen Matthew Arnold keeled over, in April 1888, while hurrying to catch the Liverpool tram, Walt Whitman managed to contain his grief. "He will not be missed," Whitman told a friend. Arnold reaffirmed all that was "rich, hefted, lousy, reeking with delicacy, refinement, elegance, prettiness, propriety, criticism, analysis." He was, in short, "one of the dudes of literature." Whitman probably figured that his own gnarly hirsuteness would save him from becoming a dude. He was wrong, and therein lies a lesson for all hardworking scribblers. Stick around long enough, develop a cult following, gain the approval of one or two literary dudes (in Whitman's case: Henry James, Ezra Pound, and F. O. Matthiessen), and you, too, can become respectable.

Of course, it's one thing for a poet who contains multitudes to become a literary dude; it's another for writers who deal with lawmen, criminals, private detectives, spies, aliens, ghosts, fallen heroines, and killer cars. Such writers—commercial and genre novelists—aim at delivering less rarefied pleasures. And part of the pleasure we derive from them is the knowledge that we could be reading something better, something that, in the words of Arnold, reflects "the best that has been thought and said in this world."

For the longest time, there was little ambiguity between literary fiction and genre fiction: one was good for you; one simply tasted good. You could either go to an amusement park or trundle off to a museum, ride a roller coaster or stroll among the Flemish masters. Genre writers were not exactly unmindful of this. In 1901, G. K. Chesterton, the creator of the plump, priestly sleuth Father Brown, lamented, "Many people do not realize that there is such a thing as a good detective story; it is to them like speaking of a good devil."

But good devils make for good company, and, in time, bookish people did begin to speak of them. In 1929 the eminent Milton scholar Marjorie Nicolson, the first female president of Phi Beta Kappa, described a dinner party rescued from the brink of dullness when the desperate hostess asked a distinguished scholar to name "the most significant book of recent years." The great man replied, "I never can make up my mind between *The Bellamy Trial* and *The Murder of Roger Ackroyd*."

Nicolson's point was not that Agatha Christie is better than George Eliot but that readers who seek out mystery novels are looking to escape not from life but from literature, from the "pluperfect tenses of the psychical novel." Nicolson was speaking on behalf of those intellectuals who, "weary unto death of introspective and psychological literature," simply yearned for a good story. Edmund Wilson, however, didn't buy it. He was irritated by the giddy approval of highbrows like Nicolson and, in 1944, published an article in the *New Yorker* that contained some disparaging remarks about the mystery genre. To Wilson's surprise, he received more passionate letters than his criticisms of the Soviet Union ever elicited—so many, in fact, that he felt compelled to revisit the case a few months later.

The result was "Who Cares Who Killed Roger Ackroyd?," which dispatched the genre's big guns with seignorial aplomb: Dorothy Sayers's *The Nine Tailors* was "one of the dullest books I have ever encountered in any field"; Margery Allingham's *Flowers for the Judge* was "completely unreadable." Reading mysteries, Wilson concluded, "is a kind of vice that, for silliness and minor harmfulness, ranks somewhere between crossword puzzles and smoking." He admitted that John Dickson Carr had a descriptive gift and that Raymond Chandler wrote well, though he remained "a long way below Graham Greene." Chandler wasn't pleased. "Literature is bunk," he retorted, propagated by "fancy boys, clever-clever darlings, stream-of-consciousness ladies and gents, and editorial novelists"—in other words, a bunch of literary dudes.

Nonetheless, it was a senior literary dude, W. H. Auden, who pointed Chandler canonward. In "The Guilty Vicarage," his sin-soaked defense of the detective story, Auden decided that Chandler's "powerful but extremely depressing books should be read and judged, not as escape literature, but as works of art." Although properly gratified by Auden's estimation, Chandler protested that he didn't know what to make of it. He had studied the classics at the Dulwich College preparatory school in London, and regarded himself as "just a fellow who jacked up a few pulp novelettes into book form."

For all that, it was Chandler's blend of stylish wit and tough-guy sentimentality that made it easier for the commercial writers who followed. If you were good—maybe not

Chandler good, but good enough—you could find a booster among the literati. In 1965, Kingsley Amis compiled his *James Bond Dossier*, and six years later Eudora Welty gushed over Ross Macdonald's *Underground Man* on the front page of the *New York Times Book Review*. In 1989, fans of Robert B. Parker's Spenser books were treated to a laudatory piece in the *Book Review* by the esteemed critic and biographer R. W. B. Lewis, and, more recently, the *Times* ran a feature on Lee Child, who writes bestselling thrillers. Indeed, scores of novelists in a variety of genres—P. D. James, Ruth Rendell, John Le Carré, Donald Westlake, Charles McCarry, Henning Mankell, Philip K. Dick, Dennis Lehane—routinely receive glowing write-ups in major newspapers and literary venues.

The doyen of thriller writers, however, continues to be the Detroit-based novelist Elmore Leonard. Leonard began publishing in the 1950s and produced at least one novel every two years. Hollywood discovered him before the book critics did (*3:10 to Yuma*, *Hombre*, and *Valdez Is Coming* were all adapted for the screen), but in short order Leonard's cut-to-the-chase dialogue, intelligently spare narrative, tight-lipped heroes, and offbeat villains had reviewers tripping over their own superlatives. In 1995 Martin Amis dubbed him "a literary genius who writes re-readable thrillers," and who "possesses gifts— of ear and eye, of timing and phrasing—that even the most indolent and snobbish masters of the mainstream must vigorously covet." It seems we have reached a point when Robert Graves's words about Shakespeare can also be applied to Leonard: The remarkable thing about him is that he is "really very good, in spite of all the people who say he is very good." Does this sound like a guilty pleasure?

Praise can be seductive, and writers who ordinarily would not reach for literary laurels may start hankering after them.

But if a writer of a romance or a mystery succeeds in deepening her narrative, does the guilt disengage from the pleasure, and is the pleasure any the less for it? Writers like P. D. James pride themselves on rejecting the very conventions of detective fiction that appealed to Marjorie Nicolson. In 1981, James enlisted the *Times Literary Supplement* to make her case: "The modern detective story has moved away from the earlier crudities and simplicities. Crime writers are as concerned as are other novelists with psychological truth and the moral ambiguities of human action."

James's point is well taken, but for many genre practitioners there is a danger in earnestness. Nothing bogs down a pulpy tale faster than real-life feelings about real life. The weakest parts of Robert Parker's violent but often charming Spenser novels are the soul-searching conversations between the detective and his shrink girlfriend, Susan Silverman. The dialogue makes your head explode, and not in a good way.

Skilled genre writers know that a certain level of artificiality must prevail, lest the reasons we turn to their books evaporate. It's plot we want and plenty of it. Heroes should go up against villains (sympathetic or hateful); love should, if possible, win out; and a satisfying sense of closure and comeuppance should top off the experience. Basically, a guilty pleasure is a fix in the form of a story, a narrative cocktail that helps us temporarily forget the narratives of our own humdrum lives. And, for not a few readers, there's the additional kick of feeling that they're getting away with something. Instead of milking the cows or reading the *Meno*, they're dallying somewhere with *Fifty Shades of Grey*.

So, despite the best efforts of literary theorists, the concept of guilty pleasures, although wobbly, seems to be holding firm. NPR currently airs a "My Guilty Pleasure" segment, where "writers talk about the books they love but are embarrassed to be seen reading" and where the novelist Gary Shteyngart turned up one day to riff on the postapocalyptic sci-fi novel *Zardoz*. Although he admitted that he couldn't quote a single sentence from Jane Austen, he managed to rattle off lines from *Zardoz*, such as "Stay close to me, inside my aura."

Probably a few well-respected writers can recite passages from genre novels, and some may recognize the following:

> I had this story from one who had no business to tell it to me, or to any other. I may credit the seductive influence of an old vintage upon the narrator for the beginning of it, and my own skeptical incredulity during the days that followed for the balance of the strange tale....
>
> I do not say the story is true, for I did not witness the happenings which it portrays, but the fact that in the telling of it to you I have taken fictitious names for the principal characters quite sufficiently evidences the sincerity of my own belief that it MAY be true.

It's a pretty good story, too, about an infant raised by gorillas: a big guy, six feet three, two hundred and forty pounds, knows how to handle a knife—maybe you've heard of him? He was created in 1912 and appeared in twenty-five sequels, twelve or thirteen of which I read when I was around twelve or thirteen. Had I been any older, I think I would have known that such writing is comparable to silent-film acting, no more believable than the conspiratorial smiles and exaggerated frowns of hammy vaudevillians. The passage I've cited is the opening of Edgar Rice Burroughs's *Tarzan of the Apes*, whose centennial is being commemorated by the Library of America's publication, this year, of the original pulp novel.

The All-Story, the magazine in which Burroughs's novel first appeared, was called a pulp not because it was citrusy but because it was printed on cheap, untrimmed wood paper. But if you wanted juicy, that's where you headed, because that's where many genre writers earned their bona fides. Chandler, Dashiell Hammett, David Goodis, H. P. Lovecraft, and Philip K. Dick wrote for the pulps, and all have been ordained by the Library of America.

One hardly requires more proof of the insidious plot: writers we once thought of as guilty pleasures are being granted literary status. The man whom Rudyard Kipling (hey, didn't he also write about some kid in the jungle?) accused of having published a book so that he could "find out how bad a book he could write and get away with it" is now a literary dude. Despite the turgid prose, the wooden dialogue, and the fact that the apes exhibit more complexity than the humans, the Tarzan novels have become a solemn cultural fixation. *Tarzan of the Apes* is both "prelapsarian fantasy in its conceit and Emersonian fable in its reach," Gerald Early confidently asserts in *A New Literary History of America*. Not only that, but the "Tarzan story of man in a state of nature leads to a kingdom no less powerful than that of Milton's *Paradise Lost*, Thoreau's *Walden*, or Kipling's *Jungle Book*." Evidently, one man's Cheetah is another man's Satan.

The guilty-pleasure label peels off more easily if we recall that the novel itself was once something of a guilty pleasure. In the mid-eighteenth century, there was a hovering suspicion that novels were for people not really serious about literature. Instead of laboring over *An Essay on Man* or some musty verse drama, readers could turn the pages of an amusing French novel or even one by Richardson or Fielding. Unlike works of moral or religious instruction, novels were diverting. Of course, if they proved too diverting, how good could they be? Hence Dickens, with his enormous audience, was considered by many of his contemporaries to be more of a sentimentalist and caricaturist than a serious artist.

Modernism, of course, confirmed the idea of the commercial novel as a guilty pleasure by making the literary novel tough sledding. Far from delivering easy pleasures, modernist fiction could be an exercise in aesthetic and psychological subtlety; it was written not for people with time on their hands but for those willing to put in the time to master it. Indeed, fiction in the age of modernism became as much identified with literature as poetry or plays, and its complexities required a new class of expert readers, a secular clergy capable of explaining its mysteries. Serious fiction was serious business, and a reader might tire of it.

George Orwell was such a reader. His essay "Good Bad Books," which takes its title from a coinage by Chesterton, is his apologia for admiring "the kind of book that has no literary pretensions but which remains readable when more serious productions have perished." Orwell had two kinds of good bad books in mind. The first consisted of "escape" literature," having nothing to do "with real life"; the second, although concerned with real life, was "quite impossible to call 'good' by any strictly literary standard" and proved "that intellectual refinement can be a disadvantage to a story-teller, as it would be to a music-hall comedian." Orwell admits to enjoying Sherlock Holmes, Raffles, and *Dracula*, but can't take them seriously. He seems positively heartened by the thought that such books remind us "that art is not the same thing as cerebration," that, in effect, intelligence could be a hindrance to writing fiction; otherwise, every intelligent critic would be capable of writing a readable novel.

Today, the literary climate has changed: the canon has been impeached, formerly neglected writers have been saluted, and the presumed superiority of one type of book over another no longer passes unquestioned. So when Terrence Rafferty, in the *New York Times Book Review* last year, expressed disappointment with a novel that tried and failed to transcend the limitations of its genre, he caught some flak. For Rafferty, the book demonstrated the difficulty of finding "an expressive equilibrium between 'literary' fiction and genre fiction." Literary fiction, he went on to say, "allows itself to dawdle, to linger on stray beauties even at the risk of losing its way." That was enough to rankle Ursula K. Le Guin: "The distinction Mr. Rafferty makes between literary and genre fiction, though cherished by many critics and teachers, was never very useful and is by now worse than useless."

The presumed dichotomy also irks Lee Child, the author of a popular series of books featuring the ex-military policeman Jack Reacher. Child is indignant that thrillers might be considered peripheral to literature. "The thriller concept is why humans invented storytelling, thousands of years ago," he told an interviewer. "It's the only real genre, and all the other stuff has grown on the side of it like barnacles." And—who knows?—Trollope might have ceded him the point. A writer who can deal with murder, barbarity, and horror—with "tragic elements"—is, Trollope argued, "a greater artist and reaches a higher aim than the writer whose efforts never carry him above the mild walks of everyday life."

But, as is often the case with efforts to recognize and raise up the formerly downtrodden, a spirit of revision can lead to overvaluation. Yes, there's something to be said for John D. MacDonald's 1960 noirish thriller *The End of the Night*, but one has to wonder at the lavish generosity that led Stephen King to proclaim it among "the greatest American novels of the twentieth century," one that "ranks with *An American Tragedy*." King doesn't want to be a guilty pleasure. Having mastered the horror genre, he started contributing, in the 1990s, to small prestige journals like *Antaeus*, and in 1996 he received an O. Henry Award for a story published in the *New Yorker*. In 2003, the National Book Foundation awarded him its medal for distinguished contribution to American letters.

At that point, King had published forty books, including the well-received *On Writing*, but not everyone was convinced. Harold Bloom fumed that King was a writer of "what used to be called penny dreadfuls." The fact that the National Book Foundation judges "could believe that there is any literary value there or any aesthetic accomplishment or signs of an inventive human intelligence is simply a testimony to their own idiocy." In short, Bloom was annoyed that King had become a dude of literature.

Although dudehood seems to be conferred nowadays for durability as much as for merit, comparisons needn't be invidious. Consider two novels—one literary, the other a mystery—that begin, not far apart in time, on a railway platform:

> It was five o'clock on a winter's morning in Syria. Alongside
> the platform at Aleppo stood the train grandly designated
> in railway guides as the Taurus Express. It consisted of a
> kitchen and dining car, a sleeping car and two local coaches.

By the step leading up into the sleeping car stood a young French lieutenant, resplendent in uniform, conversing with a small lean man, muffled up to the ears, of whom nothing was visible but a pink-tipped nose and the two points of an upward curled moustache.

It was freezingly cold, and this job of seeing off a distinguished stranger was not one to be envied, but Lieutenant Dubosc performed his part manfully.

For mystery buffs, no further clues are needed: the sentences open Agatha Christie's *Murder on the Orient Express*, still in print after eight decades. Christie's writing is like that of many others in the cozy mystery field: practical, no-nonsense, bordering on cliché, with a faint didactic hum. The scene is set, a tone is established, and nothing, one feels, will come between us and the story.

Now another train station:

The two young men—they were of the English public official class—sat in the perfectly appointed railway carriage. The leather straps to the windows were of virgin newness; the mirrors beneath the new luggage racks immaculate as if they had reflected very little; the bulging upholstery in its luxuriant, regulated curves was scarlet and yellow in an intricate, minute dragon pattern, the design of a geometrician in Cologne. The compartment smelt faintly, hygienically of admirable varnish; the train ran as smoothly—Tietjens remembered thinking—as British gilt-edged securities.

The second passage introduces Ford Madox Ford's four-decker novel *Parade's End*. Ford also has a story to tell, but he'll take his time about it, unfurling complex sentences in a series of dependent clauses, with an eye toward the unique ("minute dragon pattern") as opposed to the generalized detail ("pink-tipped nose"). Christie's language wants us to settle in; Ford's demands that we pay attention (varnish *is* admirable, but who knew?), which, of course, puts any serious writer at risk—style may not be the man, but it surely makes us notice him.

The typical genre writer keeps rhetorical flourishes to a minimum, and the typical reader is content to let him. Readers who require more must look either to other kinds of novels or to those genre writers who care deeply about their sentences. Raymond Chandler, for one, professed not to care "a button" for the hardboiled form, yet he wanted to write good hardboiled fiction. To do so, he downplayed plot and concentrated on "experiments in dramatic dialogue...what Errol Flynn calls 'the music,' the lines he has to speak."

Still, he knew that certain expectations must be met, since it's the formulaic nature of genre writing (variations serve to underscore such expectations) that keeps us coming back. The reason that Wittgenstein eagerly awaited his monthly copy of *Street & Smith's Detective Story* is the same one that prompted Nadezhda Mandelstam to ask visitors to bring her Agatha Christie's latest novel. Neither one was after startling revelations about nature or society; they simply wanted the comfort of a familiar voice recounting a story that they hadn't quite heard before.

Call it a vice (Edmund Wilson does), call it an addiction (Auden's word), a guilty pleasure in book form simply means time off from heavy lifting or heavy reading. Auden, in truth, didn't do Chandler any favors by admonishing prospective readers that Chandler's books should be "judged, not as escape literature, but as works of art"—because it's only as models of escape literature that they work as art.

Many readers may find this statement condescending. I don't mean it to be. Escape literature or guilty pleasures— the terms are functionally identical—are, if executed well, achievements in their own right. When an author captures our attention, when his or her narrative grips us without making us feel stupid (guilt being preferable to stupidity), then we're reading because we enjoy it—and what's wrong with that? Ross Thomas (the smoothest of thriller writers), James Lee Burke, Janet Evanovich, Robert Crais, George Pelecanos, and Lee Child all deliver entertaining works in serviceable prose.

Moreover, they have a gift that is as mysterious to non-writers as plucking melodies out of thin air is to nonmusicians. Plotting, inventing, creating characters, putting words in their mouths and quirks in their personalities—it all seems pretty astonishing to me. The descriptions may be garden-variety and the observations about life and society predictable, but, if the story moves, we, almost involuntarily, move with it. And, if we feel a little guilty about getting so swept up, there's always *The Death of Virgil* to read as penance.

5

IT'S GENRE. NOT THAT THERE'S ANYTHING WRONG WITH IT

Some years ago I wrote a piece about genre fiction's newfound respectability which caused the digital highway to buckle ever so slightly. Despite my professed admiration for many genre writers, I was blasted for thinking that literary fiction is superior to genre fiction and for not noticing that the zeitgeist had come and gone while I was presumably immersed in *The Golden Bowl*. Apparently, the dichotomy between genre fiction and literary fiction isn't just old news—it's no news, it's finis, or so the critics on Slate's Culture Gabfest and the folks who run other literary websites informed me. The science-fiction writer Ursula K. Le Guin, for instance, announced that literature "is the extant body of written art. All novels belong to it."

Le Guin isn't alone in her generous estimate of literature's estate. *Time* magazine's book critic Lev Grossman also rushed to genre fiction's defense with an agile piece, "Literary Revolution in the Supermarket Aisle: Genre Fiction Is Disruptive Technology." Unlike Le Guin, Grossman sees a qualitative difference between certain kinds of fiction while also insisting that good genre fiction is by any literary standard no worse than so-called straight fiction. Literature, Grossman believes, is undergoing a revolution: high-voltage plotting is replacing the more refined intellection associated with modernism. Modernism and postmodernism, in fact, are *ausgespielt*, and the next new thing in fiction isn't issuing from an elitist perch but, rather, is geysering upward from the supermarket shelves. In short, there's a new literary sheriff in town, able to bend time, jump universes, solve crime, fight zombies, perform magic, and generally save mankind from itself.

Grossman invites us to survey "a vast blurry middle ground in between genre fiction and literary fiction" inhabited by the likes of Cormac McCarthy, Kazuo Ishiguro, Kate Atkinson, and Jennifer Egan, whose books don't so much transcend genres as simply collapse them. He argues persuasively that Michael Chabon, Jonathan Lethem, Donna Tartt, and Neil Gaiman have succeeded in "grafting the sophisticated, intensely aware literary language of Modernism onto the sturdy narrative roots of genre fiction.... They're forging connections between literary spheres that have been hermetically sealed off from one another for a century."

There's no question that genre enthusiasts have found an eloquent spokesman in Lev Grossman, whose own novel *The Magicians* was hailed as "a postadolescent Harry Potter." Like many readers, Grossman is fed up with benighted critics who seem unaware that contemporary fiction has bloomed into "a new breed of novel" in which "plot and literary intelligence aren't mutually exclusive." He's quite rhapsodic on the subject, declaiming that "plot is an extraordinarily powerful tool for creating emotion in readers...capable of fine nuance and

even intellectual power." Apparently, we're returning to the
good old days of good old-fashioned storytelling, disdained
by the modernists (who Grossman grants were "the single
greatest crop of writers the novel has ever seen"), who had
more highfalutin concerns. A quick side note: graduate-
school wonks may see Grossman's admiring but grudging
view of modernism as a neat reversal of Dryden's poem to
Mr. Congreve, in which the poet contends, "The present age
of wit obscures the past / ... Our age was cultivated thus at
length; / But what we gained in skill we lost in strength."

If Grossman is correct, strength in the form of story has
returned to the novel. And, in truth, a few of the writers he
mentions have constructed broad canvases, crowded with
colorful characters engaged on meaningful quests and jour-
neys. But I have to disagree with Grossman: it's not plotting
that distinguishes literary from genre fiction. After all, literary fiction can be plotted just as vigorously as genre fiction
(though it doesn't have to be). There's no narrative energy
lacking in Richard Russo, Richard Powers, Jonathan Franzen,
David Mitchell, Denis Johnson, Annie Proulx, Gish Jen, Jhumpa
Lahiri, and so on. A good mystery or thriller isn't set off from
an accomplished literary novel by plotting, but by the writer's
sensibility, his purpose in writing, and the choices he makes to
communicate that purpose. There may be a struggle to express
what's difficult to convey, and perhaps we'll struggle a bit to
understand what we're reading.

No such difficulty informs true genre fiction; and the fact that
some genre writers write better than some of their literary coun-
terparts doesn't automatically consecrate their books. Although
a simile by Raymond Chandler and one by the legion of his

imitators is the difference between a live wire and a wet noodle, Chandler's novels are not quite literature. The assessment is Chandler's own, tendered precisely because he was literary: "To accept a mediocre form and make something like literature out of it is in itself rather an accomplishment." So it is. And there are any number of such accomplishments by the likes of Patricia Highsmith, Charles McCarry, Ruth Rendell, P. D. James, Donald Westlake, Lawrence Block, and dozens of others.

Genre, served straight up, has its limitations, and there's no reason to pretend otherwise. Indeed, it's these very limitations that attract us. When we open a mystery, we expect certain themes to be addressed, and we enjoy intelligent variations on these themes. But one of the things we don't expect is excellence in writing, although if you believe, as Grossman does, that the opening of Agatha Christie's *Murder on the Orient Express* is an example of "masterly" writing, then you and I are not splashing in the same shoals of language.

Grossman's more powerful point derives from an article he wrote three years ago for the *Wall Street Journal*, in which he argued: "Genres are hybridizing.... Lyricism is on the wane, and suspense and humor and pacing are shedding their stigmas and taking their place as the core literary technologies of the 21st century." Fair enough, but how does this reify the claims of genre-loving people everywhere? It seems to me that Chabon, Egan, and Ishiguro don't so much work in genre as *with* genre. *All the Pretty Horses* is no more a pure western than *1984* is science fiction. Nor can we in good conscience call John Le Carré's *The Honourable Schoolboy* or Richard Price's *Lush Life* genre novels.

Hybridization has been around since Shakespeare and doesn't really erase the line between genre and literary fiction.

Nor should it. There's nothing wrong with genre, and when literary novelists take a stab at it, they relish its conventions and their ability to modulate them. Cecil Day-Lewis, a poet laureate of the United Kingdom, happened to write mystery stories as Nicholas Blake, and the Booker Prize–winner John Banville doubles as the mystery writer Benjamin Black. Sure, their books are escapist, but their plots don't excuse or cover for bad prose. In fact, their books can actually be better than much of what passes for literary fiction and yet still not qualify as great literature.

This seems an easy call to make, but what, for example, does one do with a book that manages to possess "subliterary" qualities of thrills and chills while offering up a high-end mix of intelligence and stylistic bravado?

> It's official, Harley said. "They killed the Berliner two nights ago. You're the last." Then after a pause: "I'm sorry."
>
> Yesterday evening this was. We were in the upstairs library of his Earl's Court house, him standing at a tense tilt between stone hearth and oxblood couch, me in the window seat with a tumbler of forty-five-year-old Macallan and a Camel Filter, staring out at London's fast-falling snow. The room smelled of tangerines and leather and the fire's pine logs.

If this isn't especially distinctive writing, neither is it merely serviceable prose. It has flair; it exudes confidence. It could be the beginning of a somber John Le Carré novel, though it's hardly that, and soon the prose becomes less restrained, much like the narrator himself. Glen Duncan's *The Last Werewolf* doesn't so much bend the horror genre as it crosses genres, borrowing bits and pieces from espionage, romance, and erotic novels. Duncan is a writer in full throttle, out to prove that a novel about a werewolf doesn't have to run with the pack.

Here, his protagonist, Jacob Marlowe, experiences his first lunar transformation:

> He ran. I ran. We ran. All persons, the plural and two singulars justified. They grappled, sheared off, bled into each other, enjoyed moments of unity. Out of the woods moonlight painted me nose to rump, a palpable lick of infinitely permissible love that asked of me only that I be *completely myself*.

The writing is sly, funny, brutal, and excessive; there's sex and gore (sometimes together), and the fact that Marlowe occasionally takes the form of a nine-foot-tall monster who feasts on human flesh actually works to justify the language's ceremonious ripeness. If Duncan feels like sounding an echo to Browning's "How They Brought the Good News from Ghent to Aix" ("I galloped, Dirk galloped, we galloped all three"), he'll sound it. If he wants to wax philosophical or sink into sensual reverie, he'll do that too, credibly so. Duncan's voice is no less singular than that of J. P. Donleavy's *The Ginger Man* or Lawrence Durrell's *Alexandria Quartet*, except, of course, for the wolf thing.

A bullet just misses Marlowe's head:

> Cognitive pile up. On the one hand I was busy cataloguing the perceptual facts—a Christmas cracker snap, puff of dust, clipped ricochet—to confirm I had just been shot at, on the other I was already past such redundancies and springing—yes, *springing* is the correct participle—into the doorway of a former Bradford & Bingly for cover.

For what it attempts and how well it succeeds, *The Last Werewolf* is a wonderful book without being a great book. There's no harm in saying this. Most novels should be so lucky. Not that this will satisfy those readers who think that genre, if carried off with panache, deserves the name of literature. Perhaps so in very special cases, but we know where the impulse comes from: without a canon of Great Books, the guardians of culture have nothing to declare, and every reader enters the world of literature as the creator of his or her own canon, a person whose tastes cannot be impeached. This is nicely demotic, but why should readers be exempt from the same level of familiarity or expertise that characterizes aficionados of tennis or opera or any activity that requires proficiency? Reading and reacting to books may be a private experience, but that doesn't mean that all experiences in terms of appreciation are equal.

Quality comes in different forms: there is Cole Porter and there is Prokofiev; the Beatles and Bach; Savion Glover and Mikhail Baryshnikov—the difference between them is not one of talent or proficiency but of sensibility. When I pick up a novel with a semi-lupine protagonist, like *The Last Werewolf*, I'm expecting darkness, but not *Heart of Darkness*. And I'm not disappointed. Matter of fact, Duncan's foray into horror is so intelligently and exuberantly rendered that the snootiest of readers might forgive himself for letting Robert Musil and W. G. Sebald languish on the shelves.

Good writers, it bears saying, dress their work out differently. George Eliot and George Simenon both have their pleasures, just as Beethoven's late Quartets and the Beatles singing "Roll Over Beethoven" do. We can enjoy both, but that doesn't mean they deserve the same kind of admiration. Although we now shun the word "elitist," its elision signals less a leveling of communal taste than a loss of specificity. To state the obvious: popular culture is popular because it appeals to the general population. High culture, which may borrow from everything (high, low, and points in between), keeps its own company; it accepts our love but does not seek it. Yes, Dorothy, there is a high culture, even if it began as popular entertainment like Dickens or opera. The fact that something transcends popular taste doesn't prove or disprove its worth.

Readers naturally have a right to choose their pleasures, but to prefer Donald Westlake's *The Fugitive Pigeon* to Henry James's *Wings of the Dove* is not a negligible bias. That said, one should stick to one's bias. In short, "genre" is not a bad word, although perhaps the better word for medicore novels that taxonomically register as genre is simply "commercial." Born to sell, these novels stick to the trite and true, relying on stock characters whose thoughts spool out in Lifetime platitudes. There will be exceptions, as there are in every field, but, for the most part, the standard commercial novel isn't going to break the sea frozen inside us. If this sounds condescending, so be it.

Commercial novels, in general, whether they're thrillers or romance or science fiction, employ language that is at best undistinguished and at worst characterized by a jejune mentality and a tendency to state the obvious. Which is not to say that literary novels, as more than a few readers pointed out to me, don't contain a surfeit of decorative description, elaborate psychologizing, and gleams of self-conscious irony. To which I say: So what?

One reads Conrad and James and Joyce not simply for their way with words but for the amount of felt life in their books. Great writers hit us over the head because they present characters whose imaginary lives have real consequences (at least while we're reading about them), and because they see the world in much the way we do: complicated by surface and subterranean feelings, by ambiguity and misapprehension, and by the misalliance of consciousness and perception. Writers who want to understand why the heart has reasons that reason cannot know are not going to write horror tales or police procedurals. Why say otherwise? Elmore Leonard, Ross Thomas, and the wonderful George MacDonald Fraser craft stories that every discerning reader can enjoy to the hilt—but make no mistake: good commercial fiction is inferior to good literary fiction in the same way that Santa Claus is inferior to Wotan. One brings us fun or frightening gifts, the other requires—and repays—observance.

6

LISTING TOWARD
OBLIVION

Something there is that loves a list, loves it for its formality, order, and concision. Loves it perhaps out of necessity because it makes the world a more convenient place to live. From its formal inception in ancient Sumer, where magistrates inventoried harvests on baked clay tablets, we have depended on lists to codify, clarify, enlighten, and amuse, though there's not much humor in Hammurabi's code of laws or the Ten Commandments.

Writers, of course, have always been drawn to lists, if only as an excuse to parade their knowledge. There you are happily reading along in a poem or a novel when suddenly a Catalogue, an Inventory, a Phalanx of Facts appears on the page. Do writers ever consider the possibility that a list stops the action, that it gets in the way of the story? Of course not; writers don't care about *our* comfort level, they have their own agendas.

If I were to draw up a list of all the poets and novelists who have resorted to lists, you'd be astonished. Luckily, others have done the job for me, and if you take the time to peruse their books you'll see that many scribblers, despite my misgivings, can make a list practically shimmy off the page. The books I have in mind are Francis Spufford's *The Chatto Book of Cabbages and Kings: Lists in Literature* (1989), whose introduction should be on the list of the best things written about lists, and Robert E. Belknap's excellent study *The List: The Uses and Pleasures of Cataloguing* (2004), which is essentially a meditation on lists in nineteenth-century American literature. Apparently, these volumes were not enough to satisfy the public's yearning for a longer list of books about lists; and so now we also have Umberto Eco's beautifully illustrated survey, *The Infinity of Lists* (2009), which views lists as philosophically charged artifacts, and Liza Kirwin's *Lists: To-Dos, Illustrated Inventories, Collected Thoughts, and Other Artists' Enumerations* (2010), which reproduces bits of art-world ephemera.

The great list-makers (and I limit myself to only a few) are Rabelais, Montaigne, Sir Thomas Browne, Coleridge, Melville, Whitman, Joyce, Beckett, Nabokov, and Borges, all of whom have the privilege of belonging on a list of authors who have added to the store of literature. I refer, of course, to the canon of Great Books, which began to be compiled in the eighteenth century and was officially registered by encyclopedias and universities near the middle of the twentieth century. Any list is by definition a curtailment: it excludes far more than it includes. The best, the worst, the highest, the lowest, the hardest, the easiest—these practically beg for refutation. What list, after all, is complete or completely true? You'd need to have access to the mind of God to answer that question, and God, I'm afraid, is not on everyone's list of things that are complete or completely true.

Lists can be instructive, entertaining, and protean, which is not to say that every writer carries them off with aplomb.

There *is* a danger in literary list-making; it may not be on the order of flawed cape work in the bullring, but lists can try a reader's patience. Consider one of the most famous aggregates in literature. After decrying his inability to name all the Greek chieftains who voyaged to Troy ("not if I had ten tongues and ten mouths"), Homer still manages to cite in *The Iliad*, according to my count, 265 lines' worth. And speaking of Homer and heroes, whoever bothered to count the "Irish heroes and heroines of antiquity" in Joyce's nutty list in *Ulysses*, which, in addition to Cuchulin and John L. Sullivan, also mentions: Captain Nemo, Tristan and Isolde, the first Prince of Wales, Lady Godiva, The Lily of Killarney, Balor of the Evil Eye, and the Queen of Sheba. Nor do lists have to be of elephantine length to confound us. Readers, for example, who don't care enough to tell the forest from the trees may find themselves stymied by Edmund Spenser's arboreal assemblage in *The Faerie Queene*. And let's be honest, would it matter if there were four or five fewer names on the list of guests who attended Gatsby's lavish parties?

That said, there is something reassuring about a list, a precision and formality that makes us think we've got a handle on things. Isn't every list in reality a ceremonial flourish against amnesia and chaos? Indeed, before Copernicus and Kepler stretched the sidereal canvas, lists were the logical means of representing the analogical, immutable, and hierarchical universe. Nature, after all, was once a series of graded entities from the lowest (grubs) to the highest (God), and a list—whether of elements or angels—automatically conveyed the Aristotelian notion of a place for everything and everything in its place. Even after astronomers abandoned the notion of a closed Ptolemaic universe, hierarchical thinking was not abandoned. Order wasn't something you tossed aside because of a little thing like infinity. A list spoke the volumes that numbers could only symbolize.

If you wanted to tell people what you knew, you put it in list form. In his *Castel of Helth* (1534), Sir Thomas Elyot knew that melancholics had to avoid hard cheeses, beans, laxatives, red wine, coarse bread, dry winds, and the company of women. Women, it appears, have always inspired men to roll out lists. Chaucer adduced the power of love in "The Franklin's Tale" by considering all the women who killed themselves rather than submit to lechery. And Benjamin Franklin, in a 1745 letter, proffered eight reasons for conducting a liaison with older women: "When women cease to be handsome, they study to be good," "The sin is less," "They are so grateful!!" (*his* exclamation points, by the way).

"List," borrowed from the French word *liste*, first turns up, in the modern sense, in *Hamlet*, when Horatio reports that Fortinbras has "sharked up a list of landless resolutes"—i.e., indiscriminately put together a makeshift army. Anyone already aware of this is probably familiar with Keats's manifest of delicacies from "The Eve of St. Agnes"; Edgar Allan Poe's catalog of books, suggestive of a diseased mind, in Roderick Usher's library; Rupert Brooke's itemization of things he loves in "The Great Lover"; Nabokov's account of the scenic spots visited by Humbert Humbert and his fetching companion during their interstate wanderings; Cole Porter's anthem of highs and lows in "You're the Top" (Mahatma Gandhi, Napoleon Brandy, the National Gallery, Garbo's salary, turkey dinner, the time of a Derby winner); and, of course, the Lord

High Executioner's list of people who would never be missed in Gilbert and Sullivan's *Mikado*: ("I've got a little list—I've got a little list / Of social offenders who might well be underground,...people who have flabby hands and irritating laughs,...apologetic statesmen of a compromising kind"). Lady novelists, incidentally, may wish to hear no more of the executioner's song.

Unlike most compilers of literary lists, I'm something of a purist when it comes to their composition. In contrast to Spufford, Belknap, and Eco, who are too welcoming of any and all sequential material, I believe a list should aspire to "listhood." No descriptive rendering of a great warrior's shield for me, or "the types and symbols of eternity" metered out in Wordsworth's "Prelude." Give me instead the loud, unabashed shouter-outers of lists: Swift's reckoning of scoundrels absent from the land of the Houyhnhnms, or Henry Reed's decisive dismantling of a rifle in "Naming of Parts." I'm not suggesting that every list needs an interior logic (the glue may simply be the author's mind), but a true list, whether pragmatic, ornamental, or downright silly, ought at least to *look* like a list. The fact is, if you broaden the word's meaning, just about everything is a list: the binary numbers that program a computer; the DNA that programs our temperament; even the words I'm writing here. Check out Donald Barthelme's story "The Glass Mountain," in which all the sentences are numbered and vertically stacked.

The first truly modern list could very well be Arthur Rimbaud's recitation of favorite things in *A Season in Hell* (1873): "Absurd paintings, door panels, stage sets, backdrops for acrobats, sign boards,...outdated literature, Church Latin, misspelled erotic books, novels of grandmothers." No underlying order here or columnar progression. What we get instead is Rimbaud's oddly stocked mind, in which disparate elements jostle one another, collage-like, on the page.

The great contemporary list maker, of course, is Borges, who, in his fabulous story "The Aleph," attempted the ultimate list, the universe seen simultaneously and in its entirety: "The heavy-laden sea...the multitudes of America...a silver-plated cobweb at the centers of a black pyramid...all the mirrors in the planet...a copy of the first English version of Pliny...tigers, emboli, bison, ground swells and armies...the earth in the Aleph and in the earth the Aleph once more and the earth in the Aleph." This list *is* Borges, and it suggests—does it not?—the continuing incalculable exchange between the self and the world. So we catalog as we go, itemizing things seen and unseen, as we move inexorably forward, listing toward oblivion.

7

"LISTEN TO THE SOUND IT MAKES"

Complaining about poetry is a mug's game, as Mark Edmundson recently discovered after publishing his "Poetry Slam" in *Harper's Magazine* (July 2013). Like Jeremy Bentham and Thomas Love Peacock in the nineteenth century, and Edmund Wilson and Joseph Epstein in the twentieth, Edmundson's lament about the current state of the art met with scorn and condescension. Who wants to hear another diatribe against those who write, or attempt to write, verse? Anyway, poets have always encountered resistance, either because their work was said to be irrelevant or shoddy or obscure. So why add my voice to the small chorus of dissent? The simple answer is, I miss what I used to enjoy. The more complicated answer is that "Reading it, however, with a perfect contempt for it," one may discover that "men die miserably every day for lack of what is found there."

Students of poetry will know that I am conflating (none too smoothly) lines by Marianne Moore and William Carlos Williams. Although Williams's "Asphodel" is not among his best works, Moore ably defended her art in a poem designed to question it. How many poets could do half so well today? I say this as someone who hopes to be proven wrong. Like Emily Dickinson, I read poems in the hope that one or two will make "the top of my head" come off. In short, I want to feel like the teenager who breathlessly encountered Keats's "Ode to a Nightingale" or the young adult who read "The Wasteland" and felt the prosodic world stand on its head. It's probably too late to lose my own head over a poem, but I seem to recall that even at the venerable age of thirty-eight or forty I was bowled over by Philip Larkin's "Aubade."

I bring up Larkin for another reason. Despite his own distinctive voice, Larkin had little tolerance for unruly innovation in the arts. He famously disliked Charlie Parker's "shrillness" and thought Picasso and Henry Moore clever charlatans. There's nothing new about artists disliking each other's work—Tolstoy scoffed at Shakespeare's plays and thought Chekhov's only marginally better—but it's a narrowness of vision attributable to one's own artistic integrity. Querulousness can simply be informed opinion about the limitations of particular styles or forms of writing.

So let's put the grumpiness factor to bed. Let's assume for the sake of argument that I am not another reactionary stiff who doesn't get it. How do I put this demurely? I am not unfamiliar with the tradition of prosody in English from Chaucer to Auden, and if I feel that there is little poetry around that will stand the test of time, it's not because I believe that poets lack imagination or intelligence. Unlike Edmundson, who contends that contemporary poets routinely neglect the grand existential questions addressed by poets of earlier generations, my own discontent is more site-specific, tonal rather than dispositive. In short, I miss the poetry I used to hear in my head after reading it on the page. I miss the sound it used to make.

And it's sound, the way words follow each other, that makes poetry memorable in the strict sense that it lends itself to memorization. Very little of what I read now seems truly memorable. Which contemporary poems have the staying power of Shakespeare's sonnets, Keats's "To Autumn," Arnold's "Dover Beach," Yeats's "Sailing to Byzantium," or Auden's "In Memory of W. B. Yeats"? Edmundson might say that contemporary poetry is not worth committing to memory. Me, I just think poets don't care enough about a poem's music, which means they really don't expect us to recite their poems ten minutes or ten years after reading them. It's not so much the cargo that's changed; it's the means of delivery.

Five years ago, in the *New Yorker,* Dan Chiasson delivered a thoughtful paean to the work of Rae Armantrout, the 2010 recipient of the Pulitzer Prize. After duly noting Armantrout's sure touch with language, the finesse of her method, and the delicacy with which she handles the vagaries of experience, he fastens on her strong suit. Her poems are about consciousness, the awareness of being aware, which makes them reflexively chart the course of their own difficulty: "It's the mind as problem-solving device, almost as calculator," Chiasson writes, "though it is, of course, most drawn to problems that cannot be solved." The insouciant assurance of that "of course" made me realize—not for the first time—that I am not interested in a poet's mind; it's not what draws me to poetry.

If I wanted to know what interesting minds think, I would pick up Hume, Schopenhauer, Nietzsche, Wilde, or the letters of Eliot and Keats as opposed to their poems. Yes, of course, Shakespeare, Donne, Keats, Eliot, Lowell, and Dickinson had interesting minds. That's not the point. Readers didn't read those poets just for the contents of their minds; they read them for the sound of their words. Even when poets were nominally "the unacknowledged legislators of the world," poetry consisted of lines that rhythmically fixed themselves in the mind. Do poets or readers today still take this on faith? Admittedly, I may be ignorant of many English-speaking poets whose compositions reverberate by rhythmic design— so far, however, I have not encountered them.*

Instead I run into Rae Armantrout. I don't mean to single out Ms. Armantrout; I could just as easily have chosen Kay Ryan or Stephen Dunn or Mark Doty or a dozen other poets— proficient practitioners, one and all. When I read these poets, I discern intelligence, shrewdness, irony, and humor. I often admire the elliptical shorthand of their phrasing and the precision of their lines, and I'm tickled by the concentration of appellative nouns and their dispersal in lines that seem to have no give to them. In short, I believe I can appreciate their poetry. Yet, in the end, I remain unmoved by it.

Because there is no music.

Historically, English verse, depending on whom you consult, falls into categories of syllabic or accentual stresses. Deliberate patterns of alternation between stronger and weaker stresses or between shorter or longer syllables establish a

---

* Although it seems to me that I have read a great deal of poetry over the past few decades, I have obviously read only a very small percentage of what gets written day in and day out, and so my protestations must be tempered by what I am ignorant of, and no doubt this dereliction will be duly noted.

regular meter based on the distance between accented sylla-bles. Does that mean that lines must be read with equal em-phasis by everyone? Not quite. Metrical invention sometimes follows and sometimes vies with natural speech. Nonetheless, accent and duration have accounted for the ascending or descending rhythms of English poetry since the early six-teenth century.

Generally speaking, poets manipulate natural prose rhythms, creating a base line whose recurrence in the poem gets us tapping our minds and feet. The pattern established, poets can then exercise some discretion. Although formal verse may smack of orthodoxy, a poet who has gone to school with Milton, Donne, Spenser, Browning, and Tennyson can perform rewarding variations on familiar meters and fixed rhyme schemes. You need a good ear to write verse, but only an average ear to appreciate it. And if you want to know the difference between a well-crafted poem and a mediocre one, Ezra Pound's gentle reminder still serves: "LISTEN to the sound it makes."

Before it is anything else, a poem is sound; and as auditory sensation it is connected to respiration, heartbeat, and the brain's synaptic firings. The precise relationship between the sound of words and their effect may never be understood, but at least where English poetry is concerned, the pentameter line with its piquant load of accented-syllabic stresses has influenced speech patterns since the time of Chaucer. And poets, who obviously learn to speak before they learn to write, join the sound of speech with the sounds of what they read in order to create rhythms not heard or read before. And these rhythms will be absorbed by other poets, whose different sen-sibilities will tease out still *other* rhythms that may nestle com-fortably, sometimes ecstatically, in our ears.

The retreat from standard or classical meter began when the modernist poets, in addition to having legitimate concerns about meter in general, wanted to put to rest the plangent rhythms of Swinburne ("If you were queen of pleasure, / And I were king of pain, / We 'd hunt down love together, / Pluck out his flying-feather, / And teach his feet a measure") and Longfellow ("By the shores of Gitchee Gumee / By the shining Big-Sea-Water / Stood the wigwam of Nokomis / Daughter of the Moon, Nokomis").

Nonetheless, the first wave of modernist poets didn't abandon meter; they only broke with the pentameter: "That was the first heave," Pound exulted. But "heave" may be too strong a word. Eliot and Pound, Edward Thomas and later on Auden, Cummings, Stevens, Roethke, Berryman, Bishop, and Lowell didn't so much do heavy lifting as play with established cadences, hatching new melodies in the process. Writing to the critic Cleanth Brooks, Eliot observed: "Reading your essay made me feel, for instance, that I had been much more ingenious than I had been aware of, because the conscious problems with which one is concerned in the actual writing are more those of a quasi musical nature, in the arrangement of metric and pattern, than of a conscious exposition of ideas."

Meter, of course, is varied and subtle and open to ceaseless invention. It is also surprisingly resilient, even if very few poets today rely on it. But the *idea* that poetry was free of classical restraints had its downside: many poets began to write as if there were no conventions at all, and unfettered self-expression became the rule, effectively banishing all rules. "Our children grow to adolescence with the feeling that they can become poets instead of working," P. G. Wodehouse slyly prophesied in "The Alarming Spread of Poetry"(1916): "*Vers libre* is within the reach of all. A sleeping nation has wakened to the realization that there is money to be made out of chopping its prose into bits." Silly stuff, especially in light of its timing, but who can deny that around the third quarter of the last century, poetry lost its footing—literally?

As for the projectivist poets who, *pace* Charles Olson, hoped that poetry could simulate the poet's breathing, enabling form to flow organically from sensory associations, they rejected the more formalistic elements found in Eliot and Stevens, believing they acted as constraints on poetry. Though only occasionally successful in fashioning memorable poems, the Black Mountain School, at least, embodied the idea that aesthetic revolutions—modernism, no exception—quickly grow stale. Art, after all, progresses both by borrowing from and by rejecting the past. And this, if I may hazard a sweeping generalization, is where contemporary poets go astray. What, one may ask, are they rejecting? What currents are they valiantly swimming against?

Although poets will tell you that the paradigm has shifted, that musicality is less important than the focus or sensibility of their poems, it's hard to be truly original when there are no immediate precursors to spurn or deviate from. Without something to counter, the poet's "originality" is destined to resonate only within its creator. "The poem which is absolutely original is absolutely bad;" Eliot pronounced, "it is, in the bad sense, 'subjective' with no relation to the world to which it appeals."

Yet apart from a few formalist poets here and there, poets have stopped writing in meter, and readers no longer expect the iambs and anapests that formerly arrived in two- and three-beat measures. Most poets have simply shrugged off the burden of influence, making it possible to ignore the lessons of the past without first mastering them, rejecting meter before learning how to compose in it. Yes, of course, there are exceptions: Richard Wilbur, Derek Walcott, and John Hollander have all written lines that scan without difficulty. Yet even the estimable Seamus Heaney, who was unsurpassed in joining the singularity of objects with the poignancy of moods and memories, sometimes stopped in his melodic tracks to make a point rather than let the music play on. Those poets, of course, are from a generation that took seriously Yeats's admonition to "sing whatever is well made."

But song is not a word we associate with John Ashbery and his progeny. As a result, their work doesn't lend itself to memorization. Whereas Auden and Larkin hum and whistle in the mind, contemporary "verse" usually dribbles off into nothingness. It's presumptuous of me to say it, but I don't think our poets live for poetry as much as for the act of sharing their thoughts and feelings in the guise of poems. They're forgetting that poetry is a craft and a discipline before it is a reason to write about oneself.

It's a dicey business weighing the sound of a poem against its content, but I suspect that even regular readers of poetry no longer bother to commit to memory the poems of our clime in the same numbers that used to memorize Wallace Stevens. If one believes, as I do, that poetry no longer matters to the general public, despite the number of books being published and the proliferation of poetry readings, it's because poets themselves do not attempt to write poetry that fixes itself readily in the mind. It's almost as if there's a general consensus that cadence is irrelevant. Meaning trumps rhythm; connotation finesses sound.

Poets everywhere will argue this point—vehemently. Let them. Anyone who drops in on poetry readings or who clicks on YouTube can attest to the atonal quality of contemporary verse. Some poets make no bones about this. Kay Ryan acknowledged that her poems do not start with images or sound, but develop "the way an oyster does, with an aggravation." That's a nice conceit, and more power to her. Poets should write how and what they want; but let them also be aware that their work is not, as Dylan Thomas incanted, "for the lovers, their arms / Round the griefs of the ages / Who pay no praise or wages / Nor heed my craft or art."

Not everyone has to feel the same about poetry for poetry to matter. F. Scott Fitzgerald thought, "Poetry is either something that lives like fire inside of you—like music to the musician or Marxism to the Communist—or else it is nothing, an empty, formalized bore, around which pedants can endlessly drone their notes and explanations." But it isn't, of course, so cut and dried. The poems we love may change as we change, gaining or losing intensity as we age. Auden famously observed that poetry makes nothing happen. But it does, and he knew it: it makes other poetry happen; and poetry, when it is genuine, becomes part of our intellectual repertoire, part of ourselves.

Ultimately it boils down to the personal; so let me say straight out that the exquisite spareness of poets like Ryan and Armantrout, or the roll call of colloquial references favored by Ashbery, makes *me* work too hard. Yes, T. S. Eliot and Wallace Stevens also made me work, but at least I could hear their lines playing in my head. Their poems had music in them. So what I'm asking is: Do I really want to spend time figuring out the associations between words on a page and the experiences they're meant to distill if the *sound* of the poem doesn't please me?

By "sound" I mean more than just the auditory experience of poetry. After all, some metered poems bear only the faintest resemblance to music. It is, finally, the poet's voice that calls to us: "What underlies all success in poetry," Lionel Trilling wrote, "what is even more important than the shape of the poem or its wit or its metaphor, is the poet's voice. It either gives us confidence in what is being said or it tells us that we do not need to listen; and it causes both the modulation and the living form of what is being said." The paradoxical thing about this voice is that it does not actually exist outside of our own heads. When we hear a poet's voice speaking from the page, we hear it internally: the tempo, the emphasis, the feelings are synthesized in us—which is why I prefer to *read* a poem rather than hear it read aloud (unless the reader happens to be Dylan Thomas, or Richard Burton reading Dylan Thomas, but even then it's a tossup). A poem speaking to me from the page is private and makes itself felt as no stranger's voice possibly could. In short, I have a relation with those particular words, which disappears when I hear them spoken.

The poems I go back to were written mostly before 1977, the year Larkin's "Aubade" appeared in the *TLS*. Obviously, I have read some worthwhile poems written since then, but damn if I can remember them. I'm also painfully aware that if people are still reading this, some may actually go to the trouble of calling my attention to all the wonderful, amazing, moving poems that I seem to have missed. To which I say, bring them on. But let me suggest that proficiency is not the yardstick here. Ask yourself whether these poems live up to the best of Auden, Yeats, Thomas, Stevens, Bishop, Plath, and Lowell. Do they reflect the essence of their time and place in language vibrant enough and in measures clear enough to be heard five decades from now?

Perhaps I'm a dinosaur who can't make the shift from Palgrave to Pinsky—but I take no pride in it. I'm perfectly happy to be shown for a fool. But just as people can tell a good musician from a bad one, or a competent athlete from an extraordinary one, I believe I can distinguish among poets. I have a prejudice, however. While I think there are shadings or levels of skill among accomplished musicians and athletes, I feel that a poem without music is almost oxymoronic. Either you can write metrical verse or you can't, no matter how well you express yourself. The problem is that too many people who cannot write in musical form champion others who are likewise unskilled.

Consequently, the fairly large and disparate community of poets continues to generate, as if by academic fiat, poems of such odd atonal quality that most readers cannot be bothered to listen. Again, there are exceptions: poems by Galway Kinnell, W. S. Merwin, and Mark Strand are metrically intact and easy on the ears. Those poets compose works which, I believe, nullify the accusation that the emperor isn't wearing any clothes. The emperor or empress most certainly is, but the cloth is of such fine-spun thread that the garment seems unpractical—"unpractical" in the Coleridgean sense that a poem must first be a house before it can be a palace. Forgive me for pitching my tent in the stately dwellings whose music follows me wherever I go.

8

A SAD ROAD TO EVERYTHING

Keep reminding yourself that literature is one of the saddest roads that lead to everything.

André Breton

There is something primitive in the great issues that have traditionally concerned writers, Lionel Trilling submitted in "The Meaning of a Literary Idea." Questions about the nature of thought and man "match easily in the literary mind with the most primitive human relationships. Love, parenthood, incest, patricide: these are what the great ideas suggest in literature, these are the means by which they express themselves." Completing the thought, Trilling went on to say, "Ideas, if they are large enough and of a certain kind, are not only not hostile to the creative process, as some think, but are virtually inevitable to it. Intellectual power and emotional power go together."

Fully committed to the modernist charter with its complex splicing of aesthetic and historical forces, Trilling also felt the presence of something elemental, something not easily definable or communicable. This feeling probably contributed to the Freudian drift of his later work and almost certainly prompted his own fictional sorties. More broadly, the primitive underpinning of literature also attests to the unavoidable tension between an individual's need to survive and express himself and the equally powerful need to establish communities that enable but also discourage self-expression.

Without getting bogged down in evolutionary theory, we can infer that the Darwinian struggle to procreate—because it requires some semblance of security—leads to communities that help human beings sustain themselves. Rules of conduct are established that inevitably repress some of those primitive desires which subsequently appear in literature. Thus, the institutions that define civilization also reflect the tensions in our own nature. For just as no society can survive if it allows the darker facets of our nature to surface, no society can truly function if it disowns the human impulses that helped establish it. By imposing order we compensate for the impulse to create disorder. Fascism, then, is an orderly society governed by those who secretly yearn for disorder, while democracy is a disorderly society governed by those who explicitly believe in order. All this is to say that the tension between individual freedom and the society that seeks to protect that freedom is embedded in the moral and legal codes that, in effect, repress the energies that originally ushered them into existence.

What does this have to do with literature? Quite a lot. Fiction, speaking very generally, is about the individual in society, about the expectations and conflicts that color a life when an obdurate reality stands in the way of one's self-image or desires. Novels don't have to be overtly political, but they do, in one guise or another, reflect the civilization that helped shape them, and, as Mr. Orwell liked to say, "Inequality [is] the price of civilization." Such is the invisible centerpiece of every great novel, the protagonist's rebellion or coming to terms with his or her place in the scheme of things.

Novels, of course, communicate a lot more in carrying out their design, but what seems to me beyond dispute is that literature, when undertaken seriously, is a celebration not of life but of awareness, an awareness of the human condition, which is both communal and individual and inevitably strikes a balance between the two. Each of us, then, is a fulcrum where the private and the public meet, where inner- and other-directed yearnings sometimes clash. Literature gets written because of this, and what we understand and love in it, as Erich Auerbach wrote, "is a human existence, a possibility of 'modification' within ourselves."

Such modification originally came in the form of catharsis, a building up and purging of emotion, but was eventually, as Greek tragedy gave way to lyric poetry, and poetry to prose, reduced to delight and edification. The Romantic poets then raised the stakes, opening a direct passage from the subjective to the transcendent. Yet it was only when novelists deliberately began imbuing fiction with personal, moral, and psychological significance that the individual—independent from but molded by society—came to possess an aesthetic identity. And once that occurred, the foundation of literature subtly and permanently shifted.

By informing us how we live and how we might live, the novel became the vehicle of our discontent. It allowed our suffering and suggested we had cause to suffer, and, if I may reach a bit, it helped us to survive. In its own formative way, literature is an adaptive tool that keeps pace with the small and gradual gestations of the human mind. Although a great novel can be a loose, baggy monster or as spare as a lama's bedroom, its literary status rests on an ability to imagine the lives of men and women in light of the societal conditions that animate them. If it works, if it's serious, the narrative—whatever form it takes—edges ineluctably toward a realism in which individual destiny has meaning (even when it's represented to have none).

Literature, then, does not consist of everything that gets written or published, but is special by reason of the circumstances that produced it, which include the history that led up to it and the history of the person who conceived it. Fixed in time but set free by imagination, it charts our changing relationship to the issues that intrigue us: "Whence and whither, birth and death, fate, free will, and immortality," which Trilling believed "were never far from systematic thought." Literature is where we go to identify ourselves, where we shake off outmoded attitudes and beliefs, where we pause to evaluate our progress.

The only mandate here is one of exploration. Writers have an obligation to interrogate reality, to make sure that our relation to the world is or is not what it appears to be. This sounds rather grand but can be accomplished in a number of ways: through layered Shakespearian rhetoric, nuanced Chekhovian observation, lengthy Proustian ruminations, collagist Joycean soliloquies, or minimalist Carveresque touches. What it boils down to is an intelligent appraisal of the nature of things, including our humanity, which, if we're honest, contains a good dose of ignorance. What is the meaning of existence? What are we or the universe doing here? In this capacity, literature is often a wondering, an attempt to get to the bottom of things, or, at least, a faithful, if oblique, portrayal of how things are. That's why writers at peace with themselves or who just want to cobble together readable books aren't going to offer "a possibility of modification within ourselves."

Does this mean that *every* writer has to effect a change in *every* reader? Not at all. Nor must every writer, as Cyril Connolly urged, produce a masterpiece. Nonetheless, critics should know which books make the grade and which don't. This needs saying every so often because too many books are given a free pass by readers and reviewers alike. Although Edmund Wilson was griping about the number of fawning reviews eighty years ago, imagine his amazement at a literary culture where the canon has been toppled, where poets of no particular lyric skill are laureates in the making, and where the distinction between genre and literary has all but disappeared.

But as hard as Wilson was on most books, he was a waffler compared to his ex-friend Nabokov. While Wilson famously scorned the mystery and detective tale, Nabokov ripped into any writer whose prose didn't measure up to his stringent demands. Middlebrow fiction with intellectual pretensions especially enraged him. He termed such books *poshlust*, a play on the Russian *poshlost*, meaning trivial, banal, vulgar, and mediocre. Like Orwell, Nabokov didn't mind the obviously cheap or superficial (Superman, for example, was OK), but he despaired of those bestselling "stirring, profound and beautiful" novels that get "poshlustily reviewed" and reinforce and disseminate "the falsely important, the falsely beautiful, the falsely clever, the falsely attractive." In short, he preferred to sit down with Ross Thomas rather than Thomas Mann, whom he unfairly called "this ponderous conventionalist, this tower of triteness."

What irritated Nabokov was less the product than its critical reception. Too many novels, he thought, were a facile mimicry of aesthetic and intellectual values that fooled us into thinking we were reading something important. Although Nabokov could be spectacularly intolerant of some very capable writers, he had a point. One shouldn't confuse the good with the great or pretend that competence is anything more than that. Because what's at stake is not only how we regard the novel; it's the regard we have for ourselves and the predicament we find ourselves in.

What that predicament is depends in no small part on who you are and how much significance you allot to those large ideas that Trilling discerned in literature. If words such as "beauty," "meaning," and "morality" seem extraneous or irrelevant, if the prospect of your death and the death of others doesn't overtrouble you, if the phrasing of a sentence or the parsing of a thought doesn't interest you, then it's a good bet that many poems and novels aren't going to end up in your mental attic. Terry Eagleton, who bravely wrote a book titled *The Meaning of Life*, naturally considers the meaning of death: "To live in an awareness of our mortality is to live with realism, irony, truthfulness, and a chastening sense of our finitude and fragility. In this respect at least, to keep faith with what is most animal about us is to live authentically." Sounds like a pretty fair definition of the novel to me.

Nonetheless, it's foolish to think that the human condition troubles everyone or that everyone loves or admires great writing. More immediate concerns perturb us: the blatant inequities found in many societies, the nasty disruptions that rattle our personal lives, the malapropisms of news anchors. That said, one must also acknowledge those readers who open a book because they, like Eagleton, believe that there is something beyond our troubles and our blessings—and it isn't God and it isn't Art. To put it in the starkest terms possible, there's something both very wrong and very right with just being alive, a feeling that weighs not only on philosophers but on anyone who looks around and *thinks*. And it doesn't need a writer or a philosopher to bring it home. "The world is a hellish place," Tom Waits said, "and bad writing is destroying the quality of our suffering."

"We tell stories in order to live," Joan Didion wrote. Maybe so; we certainly can't seem to hold back from telling them. The truest story ever told is the one about the generation that passeth away and the generation that cometh. The most imaginative one is about God and eternal life. The rest are just details. But Lord what these details amount to. Now, one can approach these details in Wodehousian fashion: "What a queer thing Life is! So unlike anything else, don't you know, if you see what I mean." Or one can be Proustian in confronting them or Jamesian or Lawrentian or Faulknerian or Dostoevskian, et cetera, so long as intelligence and awareness are driven by dramatic sensitivity and vibrant use of language, by that conflation of intellect and emotion.

The point is—to repeat—an interrogation of life, one's own and others'. The interrogation can be dilatory, amusing, nuanced, philosophical, or earnest; it can address love, war, family life, friendship, society, or solitude. It can be driven by fear, loneliness, hatred, despair, ambition, self-loathing, or ennui. It can even be a feeling we don't recognize or wish to admit to: "The truth is that every intelligent man, as you know, dreams of being a gangster and of ruling over society by force alone," Camus wrote in *The Fall.* "What does it matter, after all, if by humiliating one's mind one succeeds in dominating every one? I discovered in myself sweet dreams of oppression." Whatever the case, literature stems from an existential dissatisfaction with life itself, with that infernal irresolution of observation and meaning, of knowing and truth. And the truth is, a mind at peace is not going to create a masterpiece of literature; it simply won't feel the need to.

There is, of course, more than one kind of literature, and aside from some flagrant but temporary omissions from the canon (*Moby Dick* and *The Great Gatsby*, for example, were denied entry for decades), we pretty much know a great book when we see it, even if we disagree about its merits. We also, I believe, know which books strive for greatness and which strive for something less. That many writers choose to tell stories from a cloistered fictive cranny or send their characters into elaborate fantastical realms is as valid as any earnest attempt to write another *Brothers Karamazov.* The question is: Should their works be judged alongside Dostoevsky's?

Literature's borders have always been porous, but it's only recently that those borders are being rubbed away. In a piece in the *New York Review of Books* (July 19, 2014), Tim Parks makes the point that "for better or worse, almost all distinction between the way different kinds of novels are presented has largely disappeared."

> Newspapers review Dan Brown, Alice Munro, J. K. Rowling, and Orhan Pamuk with equal solemnity, attention being driven by the sense that the writer is winning prizes or

moving copies or being pushed as the book of the season by
a major publisher, not by a lucid curiosity for whatever may
be written between the covers. At the same time serious
publishing houses have discovered the trick of packaging
genre fiction as if it was great literature; one thinks of the
prestigious Italian publisher Adelphi, reissuing all seventy-
five of Simenon's Maigret novels in very much the same
format and with the same $25 price tag as their editions of
Thomas Bernhard, Sándor Márai, or Nabokov.

For Parks the current state of things comes down to this:
book sales drive critical reception, not the other way around,
and at the same time, many so-called literary successes are, in
fact, not selling as well as one might think. He also professes
not to worry about "the blurring of lines between literary and
genre fiction." This I find more troublesome, not because genre
fiction is necessarily slighter but because "literariness" itself
is now being touted as a genre in both the academy and the
general press. Literary work is not a genre. You can't have bad
literary writing in the same way that you can have bad mysteries or bad science fiction, because then it wouldn't be
literary.

Although any definition of literature will be inconclusive,
it doesn't mean that literature as a category doesn't exist. At
some point in our history, language in the form of poems and
stories was harnessed to explain the world to the self and the
self to the world. After that, literature could not in good conscience be seen as arbitrary but rather as something which
answers a basic human need: it's part of the civilizing process,
it helps us to thrive. Literature may not exactly be indispensable, but, in retrospect, it does seem inevitable.

Like music, drawing, or sculpture, literature makes life more manageable; but unlike the other arts it speaks to us in the way we speak to each other; it's the self-conscious repository of consciousness. And though many minor novels, poems, plays, and essays also serve a purpose by distracting and entertaining us, we shouldn't mistake pleasure for meaningful achievement. It's simply a matter of making distinctions. The house of books has many rooms, and not all are showcases of wit, wisdom, and nuance. There are very smart writers who don't write canonical works, and there are literary writers who may state the obvious, sometimes infelicitously.

But behind all memorable work is a presiding *literary* intelligence, an intelligence that makes Shakespeare and Milton, Chekhov and Kafka, for all their manifest differences, worth studying; it's what raises their voices above others. As much as serious writers want to attract an audience, they also want to be original. So they dutifully acquaint themselves with tradition, the better to carve out their own unique place in it; and it's that elusive combination of learning, intelligence, purpose, phrasing, rhythm, and discernment that enables them to do so. What these writers read informs their work, just as the books *we* read inform our response to that work.

It's almost no use to peruse certain poems and novels without at least some knowledge of the tradition from which they emerge. To do less is to ignore the reason they exist in the first place. They exist because artists are selfishly intent on creating something that doesn't look or sound like anything else. Readers, too, are selfish in the sense that we respond to books because they reflect or confirm our own understanding of experience. And because, ultimately, each of us experiences alone, reading a poem or novel is part of the solitude that is ourselves; and solitude, as Philip Larkin observed, is essentially selfish. That's why I know better than you and you know better than me. Nonetheless, one of us might be wrong.

9

ERICH AUERBACH

The Critic in Exile

No one knows how he came to Istanbul: whether he caught the Orient Express at Munich or drove from Marburg to Genoa before boarding a ship to Athens. We know he arrived in September 1936 and was joined two months later by his wife and thirteen-year-old son. We know that he hadn't wanted to go and didn't think he would stay long. A year earlier he'd told a colleague that Istanbul State University was "quite good for a guest performance, but certainly not for long-term work." As it turned out, he stayed nearly eleven years, three of which were devoted to writing a book that helped define the discipline of comparative literature.

That book, with its totemic one-word title, represented for many of its readers the apex of European humanist criticism. The German edition was published in 1946 and the English translation in 1953, and for decades *Mimesis* was *the* book that students of comparative literature had to contend with. It didn't matter how full of ourselves or full of books we were; we felt chastened by the dialogic splendor, the magisterial command, the sheer scope of Erich Auerbach's achievement.

We may have fancied ourselves attuned to every nuance of prose and poetry, but compared to Auerbach we were knobby-headed amateurs. We had neither his philological skills, etymological training, nor his grounding in the classics in the original Greek and Latin. Although some of us (not me) were comfortable in three or even four languages, Auerbach moved effortlessly among seven ancient and modern languages, including Hebrew, which probably helped the book live up to its daunting subtitle: "The Representation of Reality in Western Literature."

Mimesis contains twenty chapters, each one anchored to a characteristic passage from a theological or literary work, which is then tested for tone, diction, and syntax, and enfolded within a specific historical context. A philologist by training but an historian-philosopher by temperament, Auerbach viewed European literature as an evolving pattern of recurring themes, motifs, narrative devices, and Judeo-Christian affiliations; and his book is essentially a history of Western literature in which successive periods are classified by the level of realism fashioned from a specific mingling of styles. For instance, Auerbach distinguished the high style of classic Greek and Roman rhetoric from the more psychologically complex phrasing of Hebrew scripture, which in turn was less graphic and immediate than the story of God's incarnation through the vessel of a lowly carpenter, which forever changed the way man viewed reality:

> A scene like Peter's denial fits into no antique genre. It is too serious for comedy, too contemporary and everyday for tragedy, politically too insignificant for history....It portrays something which neither the poets nor the historians of antiquity ever set out to portray: the birth of a spiritual

movement in the depths of the common people, from within the everyday occurrences of contemporary life, which thus assumes an importance it could never have assumed in antique literature.

If no one had made it plain before, literature, according to Auerbach, is always bounded by the writer's sense of reality which, at its deepest level, depicts everyday life in all its seriousness. "In the history of modern European culture," he writes, "there is, indeed, a constant which has come down unchanged through all the metamorphoses of religious and philosophical forms, and which is first discernible in Dante; namely, the idea (whatever its basis may be) that individual destiny is not meaningless, but is necessarily tragic and significant, and that the whole world context is revealed in it." Medieval allegory and classical decorum fell short on this score, but over time the gradual transformation of thought from the sublime tragedy of the Greeks to the tragic realism of the modern novel came to define European literature.

Mimesis, of course, was more than just a polite affront to our self-esteem; it gave us the tools to read critically and think historically; and for comp-lit majors who dovened over books between the decline of the New Criticism and the rise of critical theory only Northrop Frye enjoyed a comparable authority. Frye doesn't mention *Mimesis* in *his* seminal masterpiece, *The Anatomy of Criticism* (1957), but he, too, believed that certain scenes in literature enabled us to recognize not only the past "but the total cultural form of our present life." Frye was impressive, as were the other critics in our syllabus—William Empson, F. R. Leavis, Lionel Trilling, M. H. Abrams, Mario Praz, René Wellek, Ian Watt, Georg Lukács, Walter Jackson

Bate, and one or two more with cool Anglo-Saxon names like Cleanth Brooks and Austin Warren—but something about *Mimesis* made us look at each other "with a wild surmise." It wasn't the Pacific Ocean we were staring at, but it seemed just as vast and deep.

And naturally we were amazed that it had been composed without benefit of a proper library. Unlike other works of criticism, *Mimesis* has a backstory. For one thing, it has no footnotes—a startling oversight at a time when footnotes were de rigueur. But since Istanbul didn't have the books Auerbach needed and even fewer of the relevant periodicals, he thought it only proper to omit them. He also thought that *Mimesis* might even owe its existence to the "lack of a rich and specialized library."

The legend of the bookless scholar began in 1968 when Harry Levin's "Two Romanisten in America" examined the careers of Auerbach and fellow German philologist Leo Spitzer, both of whom ended up at American universities. Spitzer, who had preceded Auerbach at Istanbul State University, laid the groundwork in his own account of a meeting with the dean of the college, who, when asked about the school's meager library, had replied: "We don't bother with books. They burn." It was this deficit, Levin believed, that forced Auerbach to write "a more original kind of book than he might otherwise have attempted," to produce, in effect, "an imaginary museum."

But *Mimesis* was more than an imaginary museum, as Auerbach himself hinted when he carefully noted that it was written between May 1942, and April 1945, a time when the ashes rose above Auschwitz and Chelmno. For many critics, Auerbach, in recapitulating Western literature from Homer to Virginia Woolf, wasn't just shaking his fist at the forces that drove him into exile; he was, in effect, building the very thing the Nazis wished to tear down. Geoffrey Green, who devoted a book to Auerbach and Spitzer, concluded that Auerbach saw his work "as a fortress—an arsenal—from which he could wage a passionate and vehement war against the possible flow of history in his time."

This may be so, but to view *Mimesis* strictly in the combative terms of a strike against the Third Reich is to falsify its achievement. Although the occasional veiled references or the more explicit wording at the end of the first epilogue—"May my study reach its readers—both my friends of past years who have survived and all others for whom it is intended"— admittedly touch on the tragedy, that's all they do. As a defense of the Judeo-Christian ethos, *Mimesis* represents, on one level, everything that the murderers at Berlin's *Wilhelmplatz* wished to eradicate. But, let us be frank, it is, despite its subliminal opposition to barbarism and ignorance, a weak shot across the bow of National Socialism.

Erich Auerbach was born into a well-to-do Berlin family on November 9, 1892. He attended the illustrious Französisches Gymnasium and went on to study law, receiving a doctorate from the University of Heidelberg in 1913. In Heidelberg, he seems to have met Georg Lukács, Walter Benjamin, and Karl Jaspers, who undoubtedly fed his interest in literary and philosophical matters. When war broke out, he was sent to the Western Front, where he was wounded in the foot and received the Iron Cross Second Class. Afterward, he gave up law, and in 1921 he earned a doctorate in Romance languages from the University of Greifswald. In 1923, he took a job at the Prussian State Library in Berlin and married Marie Mankiewicz, whose family was the largest shareholder in Deutsche Bank. During the next six years, he contributed to scholarly journals, translated Giambattista Vico's *The New Science* with the assistance of Benedetto Croce, and finished a study of Dante, which was published in 1929 as *Dante: Poet of the Secular World*.

Auerbach was made for Dante. Everything about the poet, his work, and his times combined to win Auerbach's admiration.

> The noble style in which the poem is written is a harmony of all the voices that had ever struck [Dante's] ear. All those voices can be heard in the lines of the *Comedy*, the Provençal poets and the *stil nuovo*, the language of Virgil and of Christian hymns, the French epic and the Umbrian Lauds, the terminology of the philosophical schools and the incomparable wealth of the popular vernacular which here for the first time found its way into a poem in the lofty style.

As in much of Auerbach's work, the erudition is more than a little intimidating. One might know that the *stil nuovo* refers to a literary movement of the thirteenth century, but who can hum an Umbrian Laud?

Ensconced in the Berlin library, with his friends and family nearby, Auerbach seemed almost envious of the poet, who began the *Commedia* after being exiled from Florence. Exile, Auerbach observed, enabled Dante "to correct and overcome that disharmony of fate, not by Stoic asceticism and renunciation, but by taking account of historical events, by mastering them and ordering them in his mind." On the strength of the book, Auerbach, in 1929, was appointed professor of Romance philology at the University of Marburg, assuming the position vacated by Spitzer, who was now at the University of Cologne.

Auerbach arrived in Marburg the year after Martin Heidegger left. "He's a terrible fellow," he later wrote, "but at least he's got substance." Other faculty members also had substance, including Hans-Georg Gadamer and the theologian Rudolf Bultmann. The Auerbachs were happy in Marburg and did not think of leaving, even after laws were passed in 1933 forbidding Jews to hold public office. As a veteran, Auerbach was exempt from these strictures, and, like other Jews of the professional class, he kept a low profile, even taking the mandatory pledge of allegiance to Hitler in September 1934.

Auerbach was typical of many assimilated Jews in the days of the Weimar Republic. A self-described "Prussian of the Mosaic faith," he fought for his country as a Prussian, not as a Jew, and afterward gave his son a Christian name (Clemens) and had him circumcised, only for medical reasons, at the age of fourteen. Leaving Germany was not something he contemplated; but once the Nuremberg Laws were passed in 1935, Auerbach knew that his own exile had been decreed.

Fortunately, Spitzer, who had decided to immigrate to America, lobbied for Auerbach to be named his successor at Istanbul—which is how Auerbach found himself competing with other scholars, including Victor Klemperer, for a position that he would have scoffed at a year earlier. Auerbach prevailed, and Klemperer remained in Germany, where he somehow managed to survive. (His diary, *I Will Bear Witness*, caused a sensation in Europe when it was published in 1998.) Before he was forced out of his job at the University of Marburg,

Auerbach, still the lawyer, negotiated an official leave with the possibility of returning after 1941. The idea of permanently settling elsewhere had not yet sunk in.

Finally, relocated in Istanbul, he felt isolated but not unhappy. "I am fine here," he wrote to Walter Benjamin in March of 1937. "Marie and Clemens are reasonably over the flu . . . The house on the Bosporus is glorious; as far as research goes, my work is entirely primitive, but personally, politically, and administratively it is extremely interesting. I am thankful to [Spitzer], Croce, and [Kurt] Vossler for this solution, which was not simple to arrange." That summer the family vacationed in Germany, and Marie returned again the following year. And then, in a place where books were scarce, he produced his seminal book about literature.

Not everyone is convinced that *Mimesis* sprang Athena-like from Auerbach's head. Kader Konuk, of the University of Michigan, thinks that the story of Auerbach bookless in Istanbul is a crock. She argues persuasively in *East West Mimesis* that Istanbul in 1935, far from being an intellectual backwater, was home to a thriving community of scholars, who, in addition to their own well-stocked libraries, had access to bookstores and municipal libraries around town. Moreover, Auerbach had colleagues he could talk to and former colleagues who regularly sent him scholarly articles. He could also visit the library at the Dominican monastery of San Pierre di Galata, which owned a set of Migne's Patrologia Latina, consisting of hundreds of volumes of commentaries on the writings of the Church Fathers, which, as Konuk aptly notes, figured significantly in Auerbach's work. As for the dean who dispensed with books, it seems that he was actually a bibliophile with some sixteen thousand volumes to his name. In Konuk's eyes, Istanbul was a catalyst for *Mimesis*, a cosmopolitan city where Auerbach "found humanism...at the very moment it was being banished from Europe."

There's something too neat about this formulation, but it does suggest that Auerbach wasn't tossed into the jungles of Borneo with nothing but pen, paper, and a book of matches. Nonetheless, Konuk's characterization of Auerbach's demurral as a rhetorical device meant to stave off criticism seems excessive, if only because Auerbach's letters, written three or four years before he conceived of *Mimesis*, also lamented the absence of a "reasonable" or "usable" library in Istanbul.

Ultimately, though, exile isn't about numbers; it's about displacement. For Levin, exile was "a blessing in disguise," the very thing to have inspired Auerbach's conception of *Mimesis*. A quarter of a century later, Edward Said, the doyen of postcolonial studies and something of an exile himself, reinforced the point: *Mimesis* was not only "a massive reaffirmation of the Western cultural tradition but also a work built upon a critically important alienation from it, a work whose conditions and circumstances of existence are not immediately derived from the culture it describes with such extraordinary insight and brilliance but built rather on an agonizing distance from it."

Then again, there's also the distinct possibility that, given Auerbach's temperament and the ideas already worked out in his book on Dante and his long essay "Figura" (1938),[1] he would have produced something very much like *Mimesis* had he remained in Germany or moved on his own volition to Stockholm or Spokane. Konuk, of course, will have none of this. She insists that Istanbul was not the alien culture of

Said's imagination but was, in fact, more like home than Berlin of 1942, and that "in some sense, he found himself at home in exile."

Who can say? For obvious reasons, Auerbach probably felt both lucky and terribly unlucky about having to sit out the war in Istanbul. As for deeper motives, those, too, remain elusive. The intellectual historian Malachi Haim Hacohen actually suspects Auerbach of having an antipathy toward his own Jewishness and wonders why he turned down Martin Buber's request that he write an introduction to the Hebrew edition of *Mimesis*. In Hacohen's view, Auerbach was "a progressive mandarin" who "made a special effort to ignore" Jews while maintaining an "interplay of proximity and distance facing the Holocaust." He thinks Auerbach's silence leads readers to "find clues to the Holocaust" in *Mimesis* where none exist.

Others scholars also seem baffled by Auerbach's level tone. Peter Dembowski of the University of Chicago is disappointed by Auerbach's contributions to various *Festschriften* for German colleagues after the war, while Hans Gumbrecht of Stanford is bothered by Auerbach's unseemly hope that Germans might soon get over their guilt. On the other hand, Earl Jeffrey Richards, who teaches at the University of Wuppertal, in Germany, claims that *Mimesis* is "unified not so much by its stylistic analysis but by its underlying meditation on the Shoah."

There's something almost comical in this clash of opinion: either Auerbach pitched his work toward remembrance or he expressly avoided doing so. Could his reticence have been a ploy? Was he perhaps another Scarlet Pimpernel secretly working against the Nazis, like Rick in Casablanca, only more erudite? Richards actually suggests that Auerbach may have aided Monsignor Angelo Giuseppe Roncalli—the prelate who'd allowed him use of the library at the Dominican monastery and who later became Pope John XXIII—in his efforts to save Balkan Jews from the Gestapo.

Auerbach himself is no help in sorting through these contesting claims. Although he allowed that *Mimesis* was "quite consciously a book that a particular person, in a particular situation, wrote at the beginning of the 1940s," he was tight-lipped about his politics and didn't speak about his wartime experiences. When he mentioned current events in letters, it was usually in the most general terms. "You know me sufficiently...to realize that I can understand the motives of your political views," he wrote to the philosopher Erich Rothacker when Rothacker declared support for the National Socialist Party. "But yet it would pain me much...if you wanted to deny me the right to be a German." Not the strongest of words, although it could be argued that he did oppose the Reich's policies in subtler ways.

During the 1930s, when the Reich sought to elevate Blood, Volk, and Aryanism over humanist ideals, many religious leaders in Germany traduced the Old Testament's authority in an attempt to strip Jewish history of its original meaning. Essentially Jewish, the Old Testament was incompatible with the spirit of the German people, whereas the books of the New Testament were inspired by the Holy Ghost rather than composed by Jews. In April of 1939, the Godesberg Declaration of the Evangelical Lutheran Church concluded that the Christian faith neither arose from nor completed Judaism but was "the unbridgeable religious contradiction to Judaism." The clergymen who signed the document were echoing the

Nazi propagandist Alfred Rosenberg, who blasted the Old Testament for turning normal people into "spiritual Jews," and who claimed that there wasn't "the slightest reason to believe that Jesus was of Jewish ancestry."

A Jew in Germany, even an unobservant one, must have been dismayed by all this. And, to some degree, "Figura" *was* Auerbach's response to a nationalist agenda that sought to dehumanize Jews and de-Judaize Christianity. The essay conjures up an interpretation of historical events in which the first event "signifies not only itself but also the second, while the second encompasses or fulfills the first." Events in the Old Testament are reaffirmed in their significance when they can be shown to have prefigured events in the New Testament. By tracing the etymology of *figura* in patristic literature and stressing Augustine's conception of the Old Testament as "phenomenal prophecy," Auerbach explored the deep bond between the Old and the New. And, by showing that figural interpretation "had grown out of a definite historical situation, the Christian break with Judaism and the Christian mission among the Gentiles," he tacitly linked that break with the Nazis' attempt to despoil Jewish law and theology.[2]

Mimesis, too, may have taken its bearings from German cultural politics. The book's compelling first chapter, "Odysseus' Scar," which contrasts Book 19 of the *Odyssey* with Abraham's intended sacrifice of Isaac (Genesis 22), lays out the differences in attitude and articulation between the Homeric epic and Hebraic scripture. And because the chapter pivots on the binding of Isaac and Abraham's reflexive anxiety—one of several Biblical scenes forbidden in schoolrooms across Germany—it can also be viewed as Auerbach's nod toward Jewish martyrdom. One scholar wants to take this even further. James I. Porter thinks that Auerbach was "pressing philology in the direction of something utterly unheard: a new resistant, if implicit, *Jewish* philology."

Possibly, but how do we tease apart the Jew and the philologist? Auerbach, after all, was intrigued by the historical secularization of Christian liturgy and the ironies inherent in the medieval Church's appropriation of classical learning. No other critic ever paid closer attention to "the strange moral dialectic of Christianity" and its influence on literary style, which for centuries had to juggle the eternal alongside earthly transience. Auerbach may have wanted to correct or subvert recent trends in German philology, but his central concern was the gradual transformation of Christian realism into modern literary realism.

Auerbach is simply one of those critics whose ideas seem to grow organically from the loam of their narrative soil. To follow him on his excursions around the seventeenth century ("Racine and the Passions" or "La Cour et La Ville"), or to read him recounting the history of Augustine's *sermo humilis*, the mode of expression that best conveys the reality of Christ's suffering and Passion, is to experience what Trilling called "the aesthetic effect of intellectual cogency." In *Mimesis*, a discussion of Schiller's "Luise Millerin" leads him to write:

> When people realize that epochs and societies are not to be judged in terms of a pattern concept of what is desirable absolutely speaking but rather in every case in terms of their own premises; when people reckon among such premises not only natural factors like climate and soil but

also the intellectual and historical factors; when, in other words, they come to develop a sense of historical dynamics, of the incomparability of historical phenomena and of their constant inner mobility; when they come to appreciate the vital unity of individual epochs, so that each epoch appears as a whole whose character is reflected in each of its manifestations; when, finally, they accept the conviction that the meaning of events cannot be grasped in abstract and general forms of cognition and that the material needed to understand it must not be sought exclusively in the upper strata of society and in major political events but also in art, economy, material and intellectual culture, in the depths of the workaday world and its men and women, because it is only there that one can grasp what is unique, what is animated by inner forces, and what, in both a more concrete and a more profound sense, is universally valid: then it is to be expected that those insights will also be transferred to the present and that, in consequence, the present too will be seen as incomparable and unique, as animated by inner forces and in a constant state of development; in other words, as a piece of history whose everyday depths and total inner structure lay claim to our interest both in their origins and in the direction taken by their development.

What we have here is the work of an unrepentant Marxist critic, an elitist bourgeois critic, and a critic of the Annales school; and if we look elsewhere in *Mimesis* and in the essays, we'll also find the archetype critic, the aesthetic-form critic, and the critic whose "purpose is always to write history." There is, in fact, only one word that encapsulates Auerbach's approach to literature: philology. Despite being bandied about in academic circles, philology never gained a foothold in America, perhaps because of its lack of specificity. Philology encompasses rhetoric, classical scholarship, etymology, history, history of ideas, and criticism in equal measure. For Auerbach, who seemed comfortable with all its guises, his own work effectively married *explication de texte* to *Geistesgeschichte*, or history of spirit.

As much as he was a close reader, he was also a student of transcendental philosophy. At times he sounds positively Hegelian, convinced that the process of self-realization is achieved through the realization of the process:

> For there is always going on within us a process of formulation and interpretation whose subject matter is our own self. We are constantly endeavoring to give meaning and order to our lives in the past, the present, and the future, to our surroundings, the world in which we live; with the result that our lives appear in our own conception as total entities—which to be sure are always changing.

Then again, he's just as likely to serve up delicious nuggets of biographical or sociological fact. For instance, when pondering the scarcity of extant manuscripts in the vernacular before the Renaissance, he notes the small audience for which they were intended and remarks: "Moreover the change in handwriting from the Carolingian to the Gothic script that took place in the second half of the twelfth century may have helped to make these old manuscripts seem ugly and worthless to men of later days."

Auerbach's purpose was to show how history, or more properly how the study of history in all its variables, becomes a text's mode of being: There is something in discrete works larger than the work, larger even than literature itself; it isn't something immediately definable but flows from and surrounds our changing relationship to the world. This is where the self creates itself, achieving dignity and individuality through an articulated awareness of being-in-the-world. In short, Auerbach was nothing less than a philosopher of selfhood, a philologist whose focus on etymology and style was the means to determine an historical understanding of the human condition. And because we live chronologically as both individuals and participants in the world's evolution, our literature must speak to both, and so "what we understand and love in a work is a human existence, a possibility of 'modification' within ourselves."

After the war, Auerbach began to make plans to leave Istanbul. Although he received an offer from Humboldt University in occupied Berlin, he rejected it, saying he preferred to remain "somebody who does not belong to any place, and who is essentially a stranger without the possibility of being assimilated." With the help of the German émigré network, he landed a job at Pennsylvania State University and moved to the United States in 1947. All went well until a routine physical exam revealed a preexisting heart condition, which prevented the college from rehiring him. Fortunately, he received an invitation from Robert Oppenheimer at the Institute for Advanced Study in Princeton. He remained at the Institute for a year and then moved on to Yale. In 1953 he and Marie became U.S. citizens, and in 1956 he became the first Sterling Professor of Romance Languages. Nonetheless, he remained, according to René Wellek, a perpetual émigré, someone with his bags always packed. The Auerbachs visited Europe in 1956 and spent the following summer in Germany, where he suffered a mild stroke. Upon his return, he entered a sanitarium in Wallingford, Connecticut. He died on October 13, 1957, three weeks shy of his sixty-fifth birthday.

By then, he was, at least by academic standards, famous. When rival German philologist Ernst Robert Curtius, the author of *European Literature and the Latin Middle Ages*, visited the United States in 1949, he grumbled that "one hardly hears anything but *Mimesis*." The book was soon to be praised by Alfred Kazin and Delmore Schwartz, and Lionel Trilling included the first chapter in his 1970 anthology *Literary Criticism*. Some years later, however, the ascendancy of theory began to work against the book's popularity. Terry Eagleton omitted it from his well-received *Theory of Literature* (1983), and at least three anthologies of criticism during the 1990s failed to mention it. Perhaps it was the book's presumption of canonicity that irked academics beguiled by the provocations of Derrida, Barthes, and Foucault, or perhaps it was Auerbach's theological preoccupations or his richly cultured voice that made them keep their distance.

In any event, the neglect wasn't universal. In the same year of Eagleton's slight, Edward Said, who'd already translated Auerbach's essay "Philology and World Literature," devoted a number of pages to Auerbach in *The World, the Text, and the Critic* (1983). And twenty years later, on the fiftieth anniversary of its publication, he wrote an admiring introduction to Princeton's reprint of *Mimesis*. More tellingly, Eagleton vigorously commended it in the *London Review of Books*.

Since then a cottage industry has grown up around Auerbach's oeuvre, which until recently had consisted of five books besides *Mimesis*.[3] Now there's a sixth: *Time, History, and Literature*, edited by James I. Porter and energetically translated by Jane O. Newman, containing twenty essays, only eight of which had been previously collected in English. There are, as one might expect, erudite disquisitions on Dante, Vico, and Herder. But there are also musings on Montaigne ("When he enjoys life, it is Montaigne he is enjoying"), Pascal ("Pascal's hatred of human nature arose from his radical Augustinianism"), and Rousseau ("the first who, despite a thoroughly Christian constitution, was no longer able to be a Christian").

Porter's introduction is both far-ranging and precise. I'm not sure why he thinks that Auerbach's philological roots haven't been sufficiently recognized, but his impression that "a profound consistency quietly informs the work" rings true, as long as consistency allows for thought that often corkscrews into hard-to-define shapes. Auerbach, it bears remembering, followed in the wake of German hermeneutics and romanticism. And *Mimesis*, as he conceded, is a German book "not only on account of its language," but also because it "arose from the themes and methods of German intellectual history and philology" His immersion in that tradition, supplemented by his forceful juxtaposition of ancient, medieval, and Renaissance texts, made him a little nearsighted when it came to the finer points of modernist novels, but it also made him sensitive to their fragmentation and complicated subjectivity.

As a philologist intent on both a synthesis of Western literature and the historical particularity of individual texts, Auerbach occasionally resorts to knotty, high-sounding formulations marked by an inner conflict, a pending dialectic that waffles ever so slightly. He seems to be wrestling not only with irreconcilable differences but also with irreconcilable similarities. Said sensed this in Auerbach's attraction to "the dynamic transformations as well as the deep sedimentations of history." And this, I think, lies at the heart of Auerbach's presumed detachment. Deeply influenced by Hegalian idealism, he viewed life on earth as a purposeful unfolding in which the tempo of history is continually roiled by events that occur *in* history. So, even as the world changes in front of us, it should be viewed in retrospect, since only then can such changes become part of the tempo.

In a lecture delivered in Turkey about European realism, Auerbach interjects an apparent non sequitur. After observing that the art of realism leans toward a depiction of "the life shared in common" by all people, he states: "Those who understand this should not be shaken by the tragic events occurring today. History is manifested through catastrophic events and ruptures. That which is being prepared today, that which has been in preparation for a century, is the tragic realism I have discussed." He spoke these words in the winter of 1941–1942.

Even a great critic must have his critics. Both Wellek and Said think that Auerbach might have defined his terms better; Wellek noted certain contradictions in Auerbach's attitude toward realism; and the eminent medievalist Charles Muscatine chided him for blurring "half a dozen medieval realisms." Auerbach also tended to undervalue the comic and consequently gave short shrift to both Dickens and Thackeray. He neglected American literature entirely except for a brief allusion to Pearl S. Buck. Moreover, his characterization of realism as the unvarnished reenactment of the common man's sojourn on earth is oddly restrictive. As Eagleton pointed out, everyday life is no more real than "courts and country houses. Cucumber sandwiches are no less ontologically solid than pie and beans."

Curiously, for a critic who seemed so buttoned up in his own everyday life, Auerbach wanted us to know that a strong personal element stamped his work, that his own experiences led to his "choice of problems, the starting points, the reasoning and the intention" found in his writings. Anyone looking for these experiences, however, is going to be disappointed. Although Auerbach occasionally displays an animus toward a writer, he wasn't what you'd call an emotionally demonstrative critic. There's certainly not much pain or outrage in this 1938 assessment of fascism:

> The challenge is not to grasp and digest all the evil that's happening—that's not too difficult—but much more to find a point of departure for those historical forces that can be set against it. To seek for them in myself, to track them down in the world, completely absorbs me. The old forces of resistance—churches, democracies, education, economic laws—are useful and effective only if they are renewed and activated through a new force not yet visible to me.

That new force never emerged, and Auerbach could never take solace in the future. He was a Jew outside of Judaism and a German ousted from Germany. Even his main academic interest—the flow of history through the conduit of Christianity—attested to his expatriate status as both a critic and a Jew. And though he regarded Germany as his homeland, he still hadn't felt completely at home there. Writing to Benjamin in October 1935, he refers to the "strangeness" of his situation at Marburg, where he was "living among people who are not of our origin, and whose conditions are very different—but who, nevertheless think exactly as we do. This is wonderful but it implies a temptation for foolishness; the temptation consists in the illusion that there is ground to build upon." Such awareness is already a form of exile.

It's difficult to say when exile began to define him. Almost twenty years after his book on Dante, he's still musing on the poet's ejection from Florence and how Dante "never ceased to feel the bitterness of exile, his nostalgia for Florence, and his hatred for her new rulers." This works as both literal truth and as an obvious analogy to Auerbach himself: "You are to know the bitter taste / of others' bread," he quotes, "how salt it is."

In one of his last essays, "Philology and World Literature," Auerbach sounds like a man caught between the place he was born and the life he was born into. Here, too—perhaps more than anywhere else—he seems stuck between dichotomies: "The most priceless and indispensable part of a philologist's heritage is still his own nation's culture and heritage," he writes. "Only when he is first separated from this heritage, however, and then transcends it does it become truly effective." He then cites the eleventh-century theologian Hugo of Saint Victor: "The man who finds his homeland sweet is still a tender beginner; he to whom every soil is as his native one is already strong; but he is perfect to whom the entire world is as a foreign land." Auerbach now muses that "Hugo intended these lines for one whose aim is to free himself from a love of the world. But it is a good way also for one who wishes to earn a proper love of the world." But who apart from a secular saint can acquire such love? Auerbach never did; history wouldn't let him.

10

THE SHRINKING
WORLD OF IDEAS

When, in 1942, Lionel Trilling remarked, "What gods were to the ancients at war, ideas are to us," he suggested a great deal in a dozen words. Ideas were not only higher forms of existence; they, like the gods, could be invoked and brandished in one's cause. And, like the gods, they could mess with us. In the last century, Marxism, Freudianism, alienation, symbolism, modernism, existentialism, nihilism, deconstruction, and postcolonialism enflamed the very air that bookish people breathed. To one degree or another, they lit up, as Trilling put it, "the dark and bloody crossroads where literature and politics meet."

Trilling belonged to a culture dominated by New York Intellectuals, French writers, and British critics and philosophers, most of whom had been marked by the Second World War and the charged political atmosphere of the burgeoning Cold War. Nothing seemed more crucial than weighing individual freedom against the collective good, or of deciding which books best reflected the social consciousness of an age when intellectual choices could mean life or death. And because of this overarching concern, the interpretation of poetry, fiction, history, and philosophy wasn't just an exercise in analysis but also conveyed one's moral view of the world.

"It was as if we didn't know where we ended and books began," Anatole Broyard wrote about living in Greenwich Village around midcentury. "Books were our weather, our environment, our clothing. We didn't simply read books; we became them." Although Broyard doesn't specify which books, it's a good bet that he was referring mainly to novels, for in those days to read a novel by George Eliot, Tolstoy, Dostoevsky, Conrad, Lawrence, Mann, Kafka, Gide, Orwell, or Camus was to be reminded that ideas ruled both our emotions and our destinies.

Ideas mattered—not because they were interesting but because they had power. Hegel, at Jena, looked at Napoleon at the head of his troops and saw "an idea on horseback"; and just as Hegel mattered to Marx, so Kant had mattered to Coleridge. Indeed, ideas about man, society, and religion suffused the works of many nineteenth-century writers. Schopenhauer mattered to Tolstoy, and Tolstoy mattered to readers in a way that our best novelists can no longer hope to realize. If philosophy, in Goethe's words, underpinned an era of great cultural accomplishment ("Epoche der forcierten Talente entsprang aus der Philosophischen"), one has to wonder which philosophical ideas inspire the current crop of artists and writers. Unless I am very much mistaken, the last philosopher to exert wide-ranging influence was Wittgenstein. Wittgenstein certainly mattered to every person interested in ideas around midcentury, but in the end he was co-opted by portentous art critics of the 1970s and '80s who thought the *Tractatus* could prop up feeble paintings and shallow conceptual installations.

That Wittgenstein could have been so casually diluted by the art world was a sign that the intellectual weather had changed—perhaps for good. A new set of ideas began to assert itself, one that tended to lower the temperature of those grand philosophic and aesthetic credos that for decades had captivated writers and scholars. The new precepts and axioms began their peregrinations in the 1920s and '30s when language philosophers were unmooring metaphysics from philosophy, and two French historians, Marc Bloc and Lucien Febvre, were altering approaches to historical thinking. Instead of world-historical individuals bestriding events, as Hegel and Emerson had suggested, the Annales School stipulated that unique configurations of economic, social, and geographic factors determined the customs and behaviors—indeed, the fate—of regional people. Popes and princes may have fomented wars, revolutions, and religious schisms, but subtler, more far-reaching forces were also at work, which could be extrapolated from the quantifiable data found in everything from hospital records to ships' manifests.

This focus on the endemic components of society soon found its analogue in deconstruction, which elevated the social-semiotic conditions of language over the authors who modulated and teased it into literary art. Whatever the differences among the various poststructuralist schools of thought, the art of inversion, the transferring of significance from the exalted to the unappreciated, was a common feature. To read Barthes, Baudrillard, Derrida, Foucault, and Kristeva was to realize that everything that was formerly beneath our notice now required a phenomenologically informed second glance. And for theorists of a certain stripe on both sides of the Atlantic, this created a de-familiarized zone of symbols and referents whose meaning lay not below the surface of things but out in the open. Say what you want about the French, they made us look at what was in front of our noses. Warhol's soup can didn't just fall out of the sky; it had begun to take shape in Paris in the 1930s. Warhol simply brought the obvious to the attention of museum-goers.

Art and literature survived the onslaught of critical theory, but not without a major derailment. The banal, the ordinary, the popular became both the focus and the conduit of aesthetic expression. This may be something of an exaggeration, but it's hard not to view the work of John Cage, Andy Warhol, and Alain Robbe-Grillet as compositions interested less in art than in the conceit that anything could be art. And while this attempt to validate the ordinary may have been in step with the intellectual tempo, it also summoned from the academy an exegesis so abstruse, so pumped up with ersatz hermeneutics, that, in reality, it showcased the aesthetic void it so desperately attempted to disguise. And this absence was nothing less than the expulsion of those ideas that were formerly part of a humanistic charter that derived meaning from verbal, plastic, and aural mediums.

Not that this bothered postmodern theorists, whose unabashed mission was to expose Western civilization's hidden agenda: the doctrinal attitudes and assumptions about art, sex, and race embedded in our linguistic and social codes. For many critics in the 1970s and '80s, the Enlightenment had been responsible for generating ideas about the world that were simply innocent of their own implications. Accordingly, bold *new* ideas were required which recognized the ideological framework of ideas in general. So Barthes gave us "The Death of the Author," and Foucault concluded that Man is nothing more than an Enlightenment invention, while Paul de Man argued that insofar as language is concerned there is "in a very radical sense no such thing as the human."

All of which made for lively, unruly times in the humanities. It also made for the end of ideas as Trilling conceived them. For implicit in the idea that culture embodies both physiological and psychological codes is the idea that everything can be reduced to a logocentric perspective—in which case all schools of thought become in the end variant expressions of the mind's tendencies, and the principles they affirm become less significant than the fact that the mind is constituted to think and signify in particular ways. This may be the reason that there are no more schools of thought in the humanities as we once understood them.

Obviously one can still learn about the tenets of the Frankfurt School and Prague School in colleges across the country, just as one can study the works of Marxist and psychoanalytic critics (Althusser, Lacan, Deleuze, Lyotard, Marcuse, Norman O. Brown) and the deconstructionist writings of Derrida and de Man—but the *frisson* is gone, the intellectual energy converted into historical memory. Ironically, the last great surge of ideas in the humanities was essentially antihumanist. And because the academy eagerly embraced and paraded these ideas, the humanities themselves began to shrink. For when literature professors began to apply critical theory to the teaching of books, they were, in effect, committing suicide by theory.

This is not to suggest that the humanities have been completely revamped by the postmodern ethos. There are professors of English who teach literature the old-fashioned way, calling attention to form, imagery, character, metaphor, genre, and the fluid relationship between books and society. Some may slant their coursework toward the racial, sexual, and political context of stories and poems; others may differentiate between the purely formal and the more indefinably cultural. Ideas aren't absent; they've simply been demoted. And while it is true that people in the humanities have always felt saddled with a vague insecurity—"When I find myself in the company of scientists," Auden wrote, "I feel like a shabby curate who has strayed by mistake into a drawing room full of dukes"—they also took a distinct pride in being well-read in the classics, in criticism, in the historical importance of ideas themselves.

Auden's shabby curate has not been well served by the academy. The postmodernists, by exposing the ideological codes in language, by revealing the secret grammar of architectural narrative and poetic symmetries, and by identifying the biases that frame "disinterested" judgment, indirectly opened the humanities to the more scientific disciplines, particularly neuroscience. Creating a blueprint of how we necessarily think and express ourselves, postmodern theorists mirrored, in their own fashion, the latest developments in neurology, psychology, and evolutionary biology. To put it in the most basic terms: our preferences, behaviors, tropes, and thoughts—the very stuff of consciousness—are byproducts of the brain's activity. And once we map the electrochemical impulses that shoot between our neurons, we should be able to understand—well, everything. So every discipline becomes implicitly a neurodiscipline, including ethics, aesthetics, musicology, theology, literature, whatever.[1]

For instance, psychologists and legal scholars, spurred by brain research and sophisticated brain-scanning techniques, have begun to reconsider ideas about volition. If all behavior has an electrochemical component, then in what sense—psychological, legal, moral—is a person responsible for his actions? Joshua Greene and Jonathan Cohen in a famous 2004 paper contend that neuroscience has put a new spin on free will and culpability: "[It] can help us see that all behavior is mechanical, that all behavior is produced by chains of physical events that ultimately reach back to forces beyond the agent's control."[2] Their hope is that the courts will ultimately discard blame-based punishment in favor of more "consequentialist approaches."

All this emphasis on the biological basis of human behavior is not to everyone's liking. The British philosopher Roger Scruton, for one, takes exception to the notion that neuroscience can explain us to ourselves. He rejects the thought that the structure of the brain also structures the person, since an important distinction exists between an event in the brain and the behavior that follows. By the same token, the firing of neurons does not in a strictly causal sense account for identity, since a "person" is not identical to his or her physiological components. Even more damning are the accusations in Sally Satel and Scott O. Lilienfeld's *Brainwashed: The Seductive Appeal of Mindless Neuroscience*, which argues that the insights gathered from neurotechnologies have less to them than meets the eye. The authors seem particularly put out by the real-world applications of neuroscience as doctors, psychologists, and lawyers increasingly rely on its tenuous and unprovable conclusions. Brain scans evidently are "often ambiguous representations of a highly complex system...so seeing one area light up on an MRI in response to a stimulus doesn't automatically indicate a particular sensation or capture the higher cognitive functions that come from those interactions."

What makes these arguments, as well as those swirling around evolution, different from the ideas that agitated Trilling can be summed up in a single word: perspective. Where once the philosophical, political, and aesthetic nature of ideas was the sole source of their appeal, that appeal now seems to derive from something far more tangible and local. We have shifted our focus from the meaning of ideas to the means by which they're produced. The same questions that always intrigued us—What is justice? What is the good life? What is morally valid? What is free will?—now take a back seat to the biases embedded in our neural circuitry. Instead of grappling with the gods, we seem to be more interested in the topography of Mount Olympus.

In other words, there's a good reason that "neurohumanities" are making headway in the academy. Now that psychoanalytic, Marxist, and literary theory have fallen from grace, neuroscience and evolutionary biology can step up. And what better way for the liberal arts to save themselves than to borrow liberally from science? A 2013 article in the *Nation* informs us that "Duke and Vanderbilt universities now have neuroscience centers with specialties in humanities hybrids" and that Georgia Tech held a Neuro-Humanities Entanglement Conference in 2012 because "emerging research in the brain sciences has set into motion fundamental questions relating to social, political, aesthetic, and scientific discoveries." Apparently, speech, writing, meaning, and self-image are all "entangled with neural circuitry." The message is clear: Cognition is in every manner of speaking the tissue that connects all humanistic endeavors.

"Can 'Neuro Lit Crit' Save the Humanities?" the *New York Times* asked in 2010. Apparently so, if the government and foundations are more inclined to fund the humanities when they borrow terms and ideas from cognitive science. In a 2008 paper titled "The Seductive Allure of Neuroscience Explanations," Deena Skolnick Weisberg et al. demonstrated that ordinary people's opinions were so influenced by neuroscientific terms that any explanation or critical judgment employing them seemed valid, however nonsensical.[3] Well, professors of English and philosophy are ordinary people, too.

Although I haven't done a precise count, the nonfiction books that receive the most play in our Book Reviews and general-interest magazines, aside from biographies and histories, deal with neurological and evolutionary topics. Particle and quantum physics receive their due, but the ideas associated with them are so mathematically recondite that any general discussion is somewhat beside the point.[4] There is also astrophysics, which continues to bring us the implausible news of the origin, expansion, and ending of the universe, not to mention the idea that ours is but one universe among an infinite number of parallel ones.[5]

None of this affects the price of oil or Broadway box office, but the "conformal cyclic cosmology" of Roger Penrose, which attempts to explain the mystery of increasing entropy in a universe that began in a state of *maximum* entropy, and Lee Smolin's recasting of Einsteinian relativity, whereby the four-dimensional space-time continuum is less a fact than an idea, and less an idea than an illusion (since "the real relationships that form the world are a dynamical network" evolving over time) are damned interesting ideas.

As are those found in Thomas Nagel's controversial book *Mind and Cosmos*, which had scientists up in arms because

Nagel had the gall to question the neo-Darwinian belief that consciousness, like any aspect of adaptability, is evolutionary in nature. "It is prima facie highly implausible," Nagel writes, "that life as we know it is the result of a sequence of physical accidents together with the mechanism of natural selection." Though there is precious little evidence, Nagel chooses to believe in a teleological universe with nature predisposed to give rise to conscience existence, since no mechanistic explanation seems commensurate with the miracle of subjective experience and the ability to reason.

Nagel isn't the only voice in the wilderness. There are scientists, not many to be sure, who also hypothesize that human life was inevitable. Robert Hazen, a mineralogist and biogeologist, put it this way: "Biochemistry is wired into the universe. The self-made cell emerges from geochemistry as inevitably as basalt or granite." Indeed, the tendency to think that organisms increase in complexity over time seems natural. So why not actual laws of nature to vouchsafe this eventuality? According to Stuart Kauffman of the Santa Fe Institute, the universe gives us "order for free." Kauffman believes that all molecules must sooner or later catalyze themselves in self-sustaining reactions, or "autocatalytic networks," crossing the boundary between inanimate and animate.

The more common view is that while natural selection encourages the development and retention of traits that help us to survive, evolution is essentially directionless; it has no goals, no set outcome. What's confusing for the interested layman is the divergence of educated opinion on the subject. On the one hand, you have philosophers and psychologists like Dennis Dutton advocating for an evolutionary bias toward beauty, morality, and even God.[6] And, on the other hand, evolutionary biologists like the late Steven Jay Gould insist that our preferences and biases, instead of being adaptations, derived from our oversized brains, byproducts of a physiological anomaly. This anomaly, the human brain, is, of course, all the rage these days: the one big idea capable of subsuming all others.

Twenty-five years ago, humanist ideas still had relevance; it seemed important to discuss critical models and weigh ideas about how to read a text. "What are you rebelling against?" a young woman asked Brando in *The Wild One*. "What d'ya got?" he replied. As if to make up for two and a half centuries of purportedly objective aesthetic and moral judgments, an array of feminists, Marxists, deconstructionists, and semioticians from Yale to Berkeley routinely engaged in bitter skirmishes. Yes, a few traditional men and women of letters continued to defend objective values, but it seemed that practically everyone in the academy was engaged on some antinomian quest.

Nothing remotely similar exists today. Pundits and professors may still kick around ideas about our moral or spiritual confusion, but the feeling of urgency that characterized the novels of Gide, Mann, Murdoch, Bellow, or Sebald seems awfully scarce. Is there a novelist today of whom we say, as someone said of Dostoevsky, he "felt thought." To read Dostoevsky, as Michael Dirda pointed out, is to encounter "souls chafed and lacerated by theories." This is not to suggest that you can't find ideas in Richard Powers or David Foster Wallace; it's just that the significance attached to their ideas has been dramatically muted by more pressing concerns.

What these concerns are will be a matter of individual taste and temperament. Nonetheless, no one who came of age in the 1960s or '70s can fail to notice that the gods who mesmerized Trilling have dropped from sight. And it's precisely because Trilling and T. S. Eliot were the high priests of modernism and Derrida the iconic trickster of postmodernism that we're forced to acknowledge that no literary or philosophical thinker has arisen to take their place. As for the ideas that absorb our chattering classes, they are hardly divine or intrusive. Discounting the ideological posturing of zealots and jihadists, of fundamentalists and antireligionists, how many lives are affected by an adherence to, or rejection of, humanist ideals? Recent arguments about God or creationism are old hat, despite the exhortations of Christopher Hitchens and Richard Dawkins. Lord, how far removed these trumpeting denunciations are from the nuanced considerations of Paul Tillich, Hans Jonas, and Ronald Niebuhr. That "dark and bloody crossroads where literature and politics meet" is hardly dark or bloody.

In fact, the crossroads have a whole new look to them. In April of 2013 *Prospect Magazine*, hoping to provide "a snapshot of the intellectual trends that dominate our age," conducted a poll to identify the most important world thinkers. Among the top thirty "winners" there was only one novelist, Arundhati Roy; one historian, Niall Ferguson; and not a single poet or literary critic. A sprinkling of philosophers (Martha Nussbaum, Michael Sandel, Roberto Unger) rounded out the complete list of sixty-five thinkers, which consisted mainly of economists, psychologists, biologists, sociologists, and political scientists. Aside from wondering what grand intellectual design informs the work of Nate Silver and George Soros, I attach no judgment to the choices. The more public the figure, apparently, the more intellectual his or her accomplishments.

Such is the way of intellectual fashion; what bothered intellectuals two or three decades ago is now passé. Had a magazine in 1980 surveyed the "top thinkers" of that day, a goodly number of critics and historians would have made the grade. To name just a few: Paul de Man, Edward Said, Harold Bloom, Hilton Kramer, George Steiner, Isaiah Berlin, Raymond Williams, Jacques Barzun, Eric Hobsbawm, Susan Sontag, Hannah Arendt, and H. Trevor Roper.

The liberal arts, to put it gently, are not where the action is these days. Apparently, only 7.6 percent of bachelor's degrees were granted in the humanities in 2010, and, according to William Deresiewicz's recent book *Excellent Sheep: The Miseducation of the American Elite and the Way to a Meaningful Life*, students majoring in English declined to 3 percent in 2011–2012, less than half of what it had been forty years ago. None of this presupposes the absence of important ideas, but it does suggest that the really *interesting* ideas no longer flow from the humanities. Francis Fukuyama's protestations about the end of history, in 1989, seemed more of a stunt, albeit a Hegelian stunt, than a credible vision of the future. On occasion, an anthropologist or a professor of geography like Jared Diamond has come along and put a different spin on how societies evolve—environmental and ecological factors still trump politics and belief systems—but for the most part, the ideas that engage us and seem essential to understanding how we think and function are primarily scientific in nature.

Since the beginning of the nineteenth century, the intellectual world has not been so much one world as a hazy, obscure planet around which various well-marked satellites circle, each believing its rotation comes closest to illuminating the hidden undifferentiated surface. These smaller, self-contained entities, whether they were of the scientific, scholarly, or *belle-lettrist* kind, were for the most part intolerant of each other, their orbits tracing dissimilar points of view. The bifurcation of knowledge that emerged during the Enlightenment, when philosophers argued that universal truths could be gleaned through study and reason, continued apace until scientist, classicist, theologian, economist, and alienist could no longer converse profitably about their respective fields. But except for the most introverted, tunnel-vision thinkers, intellectuals still met and collided on ideological grounds. The meaning of life, the ethical way to live, the moral makeup of society, the rights of the individual, the good of the community, the role of art were issues that engrossed all thoughtful people.

While there is no shortage of conflict around the globe today—wars, rebellions, incursions, protests—the disputes that galvanized intellectuals of twenty and thirty years ago seem far removed from daily life. The new disputations, aside from internecine disagreements that are always cropping up in particular fields, center on aspects of evolutionary biology and cognitive science. The ideas engendered during the Enlightenment regarding epistemology, government, and aesthetics no longer engage our best minds except as the problematic yield of an inherited psychological and physiological compound.

We continue to discuss the state of education, the meaning of history, the efficacy of language, and the interpretation of books, but discussions of ideological and political views seem pat and tired. A certain sameness afflicts our intellectual journals except when we speak about the brain or the meaning of consciousness. And when one thinks about what's past and what's present, it's hard to imagine someone tomorrow who could possess the transformative power of Descartes, Newton, Darwin, Marx, Freud, and, on a lesser scale, Hume, Kant, Wittgenstein, Braudel, Thomas Kuhn, or Derrida.[7]

Postmodernism, which was smart, stimulating, ridiculous, and objectionable by turn, has left us in the lurch. Having discredited the centrality of the humanistic enterprise, the postmodern ethos of inversion has forced us to acknowledge that culture, and all that culture once meant, is not a thing apart but rather the semiotic expression of society's need to sustain those in power. So hierarchies had to be dismantled; and onto the leveled playing field came poets who couldn't tell an iamb from an apple, painters who couldn't draw an apple, and conceptual "artists" like Damien Hirst who openly and cynically promote and sell non-art. Sheer frippery for the gullible.

The not-so-wonderful irony of the postmodern program was that its theoretic rigor and forceful determination to get to the bottom of things precipitated a great falling off in cultural life. Although we can't quite return to the "innocence" of modernism (never mind its many supple and complicated byways), we've also lost our appetite for locating hidden modalities in art and literature. Yet art and literature still have a place in our lives. How to explain it without resorting to the assumptive modes of criticism that the postmodernists did their best to undermine? This perceived stasis of nowhere-to-go is leading humanists back to old-fashioned methods of relying on the hard data and empirical certainty of scientific research.

If questions of art, beauty, morality, and value continue to engage us, the answers, so it's said, must lie in our genes. Or in our frontal cortices. Or in our innate capacity for wonder, which makes us adapt better to the wonder of existence. It's anyone's guess. It seems, however, that by ceding such questions to biological and cognitive science we have made peace, at least for the moment, with the ideas that used to make intellectuals reach for their pens and sometimes their guns. It's hard to know exactly what this concession means, yet one can't help but reflect that by placing too much faith in the human brain, we may be relinquishing the idea that the mind might one day fathom the human condition.

POSTSCRIPT

Looking over these essays, I have to wonder if any of this matters anymore? Is there any point in trying to defend a model of literature that now seems a Stonehenge of outmoded values and beliefs? Literary fiction is apparently a genre no better or worse than any other, and barely competent writers are accorded the esteem once reserved for Auden and Henry James. Or, to come at it slantwise: No matter how we define or recalibrate "literature," writers always spring up who continue to create meaningful work. In our own day, Alice Munro, Richard Powers, Elena Ferrante, David Foster Wallace, and Karl Ove Knausgaard write stories and books that may well pass the test of time. Why bother then to deride the age? Why criticize those who value the wrong books or who maintain that things were never so bad as when some books were considered to be "Great"?

To answer this, I have to step back and survey a literary landscape that has been eroded to an unprecedented degree. We see it in the diminishing number of book-review sections and in the authors they choose to feature. We see it in the rampaging, ill-formed opinions on the Internet. We see it in the teachers who promote formerly disenfranchised authors over the Great Books, and in the students who pragmatically avoid an irrelevant humanities curriculum. Some of this is attributable to the ordinary course of events, to generational longings, changes in technology, economic fluctuations, and to cyclical feelings of cultural affirmation and dissent. But some of it, I am sorry to say, stems in part from an effort to punish Western civilization for its historical callousness toward people who look different from those who run our cultural institutions. Only the dangerously benighted could argue that the West did not exhibit an injurious disregard for the rights of blacks, Jews, Irish, and Indians, both Asian and North American. And since the world has to pay for its mistakes, it's far easier to mete out justice culturally than it is politically.

But reparations in the form of a more flexible canon and a more tolerant attitude toward the disenfranchised contain something greater than a dedicated political correctness. A deeper discontent is felt, an unhappiness not just with the state but with a state of mind, with the assumptions and rules of thought that emerged during the Enlightenment, when, broadly speaking, educated men and women abjured the instinctive and the irrational in favor of a commitment to knowledge. Enlightenment thinkers, whatever their differences, held that "universal principles of life and art existed," as I have written elsewhere, "in the very commutation between thought and expression, principles that could be applied productively to human affairs."[1]

But human affairs didn't improve much, did they? Although the idea of progress became an anthem, and progress in the sciences and the arts certainly accelerated, the world remained a rather harsh and forbidding place, where individuals, communities, and nations continued to devise new ways of enslaving and destroying each other. What good were our writers and philosophers, our statesmen and educators, when poverty, racism, aggression, and violence remained a way of life for most people? No wonder that antinomian scholars eventually launched a critique of reason as it had developed in the West. Perhaps reason itself with its logocentric perspective, implicit repression of our natural instincts, and promotion of binary opposites (speech/writing, presence/absence) was responsible for the social and sexual hierarchies that harmed and demeaned so many.

In any event, the canon, as the child of the Enlightenment, the issue of privileged white European males, became another expression of an entrenched elite who refused to cede power to women and minorities. As such, the Great Books could hardly reflect universal truths. They had to go, and pretty much have. But if their expulsion was guided by good intentions, the rationale for such action was muddied at best. The anti-canonites either missed or misunderstood the tension that has always existed between art and society.

Culture and the arts are not the same thing: one derives its essential quality from the general, the other from the individual, and any attempt to subsume the latter under the aegis of the former obscures the purpose and nature of the artistic endeavor. Although a variety of cultural materialists and New Historicists have shifted the emphasis from authors to the society that shaped them and, in the process, highlighted the many subcurrents of popular culture that influence literature, literature is not reducible to a socialized phenomenon. It is that, of course, but it's also something more.

An original and brilliant poem or novel is not one text among myriad texts, but a unique contribution to an ongoing discussion with other writers past and present. And though the political and social forces swirling around a writer are undoubtedly important when evaluating the work, they are not necessarily integral to it. A love affair or the end of the affair, wars and hard times or, conversely, peace and prosperity, may generate and color the work, but so does everything else involved in the life of the mind. As I noted in another essay, the French Revolution may have been responsible for *Lyrical Ballads*, but does not explain it; Napoleon may have been the inspiration for the *Eroica*, but his life does not sustain it.[2]

Although literary anthropologists can demonstrate why a particular work finds favor at a particular time in a particular place, they are hard-pressed to explain why some works transcend the culture that helped produce them. For if nothing falls outside of culture, how to account for the fact that certain works last while others do not? Needless to say, excellent critics, including Lukács, Arnold, Auerbach, and Leavis, have put forth theories on the matter ranging from the broadly sociological to the predominately aesthetic, but in the end... in the end it comes down to the decisions of those in the position to make such decisions.

More than a hundred years ago, the English writer Arnold Bennett in "Why a Classic Is a Classic" (1909) deduced that a work of genius survives because "a passionate few" readers in every generation both recognize and remember it.

> These few are always at work. They are always rediscovering genius. Their curiosity and enthusiasm are exhaustless, so that there is little chance of genius being ignored. And, moreover, they are always working either for or against the verdicts of the majority. The majority can make a reputation, but it is too careless to maintain it.

One can wave away this explanation by pointing out that these guardians of culture are all cut from the same expensive cloth and have a stake in maintaining the reputations of those writers who seem to speak for them. Nonetheless, this doesn't invalidate the premise that literature is independent of the likes and dislikes of the general public. Art—unless specifically designated—is not created for the public but for those interested in art. And though tastes may differ and works fall in and out of fashion, the recognition of a natural hierarchy is something that persists even to this day.

> The one reassuring aspect of the literary affair is that the passionate few are passionate about the same things. A continuance of interest does, in actual practice, lead ultimately to the same judgments. There is only the difference in width of interest. Some of the passionate few lack catholicity, or, rather, the whole of their interest is confined to one narrow channel; they have none left over. These men help specially to vitalise the reputations of the narrower geniuses: such as Crashaw. But their active predilections never contradict the general verdict of the passionate few; rather they reinforce it.

Of course, what seemed obvious one hundred years ago is no longer the case. We have divested the passionate few of their privileges and responsibilities. Greatness is not only *not* the province of the passionate few—who, after all, has the right to declare it?—it's another false category intended to preserve the status quo. And yet we still aspire to it. Don't we routinely ascribe greatness to such ambitious writers as David Foster Wallace and David Mitchell? And not just them. If one writes enough and sells enough, then greatness, too, is attainable, as evidenced by the reputations of Stephen King and J. K. Rowling.

Although literature with a capital L is viewed with skepticism in the academy, publishers don't have that luxury. People who market books don't worry about what is or isn't literature: it's *all* literature and it's all good, and a good deal of it is "great." Practically every season brings forth a new literary masterpiece, and no one except for the odd disgruntled critic bothers to refute this. And it's precisely because the canon is defunct that so many "modern classics" now roost among us and so many reviewers extol poems and novels that only another striving writer could possibly like.

Perhaps I exaggerate, but doesn't it seem that we live in an age of diminished expectations? We're satisfied with the ordinary and competent (when we're not waxing enthusiastic over the meretricious and mediocre). The old adage that the best is the enemy of the good has fallen by the wayside, which, not ironically, makes it easier for more good books to get written, but also for more bad books to get by. So we push on, faces pressed against the screen, carried relentlessly into a future where readers who remember what literature once meant must wonder: Is this the best we can do?

NOTES

1. What Is Literature?

1. In addition to Trevor Ross's penetrating study, see also Jonathan Kramnick's *Making the English Canon*, John Guillory's *Cultural Capital*, and the excellent anthology *Debating the Canon*, edited by Lee Morrissey.

2. Between 1842 and 1896, around two-thirds of novels first published in book form in England (i.e., not already serialized in magazines) were released as triple-deckers. As for the popularity of serialization, the majority of Dickens's novels ran in twenty monthly installments, and even Henry James divided his work into matching sections, the easier to serialize them.

3. Not everyone prostrated himself before the Great Books. Dwight Macdonald objected that "minor works by major writers are consistently preferred to major works by minor writers. Thus nearly all Shakespeare is here, including even *The Two Gentlemen of Verona*, but not Marlowe's *Dr. Faustus* or Webster's *Duchess of Malfi* or Jonson's *Volpone*. Nearly all Milton's poetry is here, but no Donne, no Herrick, no Marvell, or, for that matter, any other English

poetry except Chaucer and Shakespeare....Even if in every case the one right author had been elected to the Great Writers' Club, which is not the situation, this principle of selection would give a distorted view of our culture, since it omits so much of the context in which each great writer existed."

4. Today the Library of America confers value on writers, whatever one thinks of them, by encasing their work inside handsome black-jacketed covers with a discrete stripe of red, white, and blue on the spine.

2. Prélude

1. This is not to dismiss the changes in scholarly or scientific thinking that took place during the Middle Ages, especially after the capture of Toledo in 1085, which surrendered books in Hebrew, Greek, and Arabic. Here, I mainly confine myself to "the idea of progress" and its slow acceptance among learned readers for whom Papal dicta constituted inviolable proof.

2. The history of "standing on the shoulders of giants" is a bit shaky. The phrase is attributed both to the twelfth-century scholastic Bernard de Chartres ("In comparison with the ancients, we stand like dwarfs on the shoulders of giants") and to John of Salisbury (1120–1180), who wrote: "We see more, and things that are more distant, than [the ancients] did, not because our sight is superior or because we are taller than they, but because they raise us up, and by their great stature add to ours." Also, Robert Burton's *The Anatomy of Melancholy* (1621) contains the phrase "Pygmies placed on the shoulders of giants see more than the giants themselves," and Isaac Newton, in a

letter to Robert Hooke (February 5, 1676), stated: "If I have seen further, it is by standing on the shoulders of giants."

3. In "Vico and Aesthetic Historicism," Erich Auerbach points out that both general and aesthetic historicism arrived comparatively late (in the middle of the eighteenth century) because of the respect accorded to Greek and Roman civilization, whose art and poetry served for centuries as models to be imitated, "and nothing is more contrary to aesthetic historicism than imitation of models. It promotes absolute standards and rules of beauty."

4. In the interests of full disclosure, Le Guin took exception to an article of mine that appeared in the *New Yorker* (May 28, 2015) which addressed the differences between genre fiction and literary fiction.

9. Erich Auerbach: The Critic in Exile

1. Posthumously collected in *Scenes from the Drama of European Literature.*

2. David Weinstein and Avihu Zakai describe "Figura" as part of "Auerbach's *Kulturkampf* against the premises of Aryan philology and the spread of Nazi barbarism."

3. In addition to the books mentioned here, Auerbach wrote, while teaching in Istanbul, a text on Romance philology.

10. The Shrinking World of Ideas

1. The past three decades have seen a raft of books about the brain and its indelible complicity in our lives. Among them: Patricia S. Churchland's *Braintrust: What Neuroscience*

Tells Us about Morality; Paul Thagard's *The Brain and the Meaning of Life*; Michael Gazzaniga's *The Ethical Brain* and *Who's in Charge?: Free Will and the Science of the Brain Human*; Laurence Tancredi's *Hardwired Behavior: What Neuroscience Reveals about Morality*; Sam Harris's *The Moral Landscape: How Science Can Determine Human Values*; V. S. Ramachandran's *The Tell-Tale Brain: A Neuroscientist's Quest for What Makes Us Human*; and Max Bennett and Peter Hacker's *Philosophical Foundations of Neuroscience*. There is also an *Oxford Handbook of Neuroethics*, edited by Judy Illes and Barbara J. Sahakian.

2. "For the Law, Neuroscience Changes Nothing and Everything," *The Royal Society*, November 26, 2004.

3. As the abstract in the *Journal of Cognitive Science* (March 20, 2008) notes, the "subjects in the two nonexpert groups additionally judged that explanations with logically irrelevant neuroscience information were more satisfying than explanations without. The neuroscience information had a particularly striking effect on nonexperts' judgments of bad explanations, masking otherwise salient problems in these explanations."

4. How can one understand such intriguing yet counterintuitive ideas as "entanglement" (where two electrons a million miles apart coordinate their behaviors) without the mathematical framework of quantum mechanics? How does one imagine causality independent of space and time?

5. According to Stephen Hawking and Leonard Mlodinow in *The Grand Design* (Bantam, 2010), p. 165, "Just as Darwin and Wallace explained how the apparently miraculous design of living forms could appear without intervention by a supreme being, the multiverse concept can explain

the fine-tuning of physical law without the need for a benevolent creator who made the universe for our benefit."

6. Dutton maintains that art is "an inherited physiological, affective, or behavioral characteristic that reliably develops in an organism, increasing its chances of survival and reproduction." Even the ability to distinguish truth from falsehood, according to W. V. O. Quine, is part of the evolutionary process. See Dutton's *The Art Instinct*; Brian Boyd's *Why Lyrics Last: Evolution, Cognition, and Shakespeare's Sonnets*; and Dean Hamer's *The God Gene*, among other works.

7. I'm not forgetting about artificial intelligence, which was much discussed by both computer scientists and philosophers toward the end of the last century. Still, the idea of duplicating or simulating human intelligence in machines seems to have given ground to the attempt to explain intelligence by analyzing the complex organ whose circuitry is responsible for it.

Postscript

1. See "Certitudes," in *Agitations: Essays on Life and Literature* (New Haven, CT: Yale University Press, 2002).

2. "The Worst of Times: Revisiting the Great Depression," *Harper's*, November 2009.

CREDITS

ii. Honoré Daumier's *Une Discussion littéraire a la deuxième Galerie* (1864). Lithograph. Image courtesy of the National Gallery of Art.

1. "What Is Literature?: In Defense of the Canon." *Harper's*. March 2014.

2. "Prelude—Of Resistance and Celebration." A briefer version titled "What We Lose When We Lose the Canon" appeared in *The Chronicle of Higher Education*. January 5, 2015.

3. "Should Writers Reply to Reviewers?" *The Chronicle of Higher Education*. March 18, 2012.

4. "Easy Writers: Guilty Pleasures without the Guilt." *The New Yorker*. May 28, 2012.

5. "It's Genre. Not That There is Anything Wrong With It." A somewhat shorter version appeared in *The New Yorker* (Page-Turner). October 24, 2012.

6. "Listing Toward Oblivion." Published as "The Joy of Lists" in *The New York Times Book Review*. December 5, 2010.

7. "LISTEN To the Sound It Makes." A shorter version appeared in *The Chronicle of Higher Education*. October 7, 2013.

8. "A Sad Road to Everything." Forthcoming in *The Chronicle of Higher Education*.

9. "Erich Auerbach: Critic in Exile." An abbreviated version titled "The Book of Books" appeared in *The New Yorker*. December 9, 2013.

10. "The Shrinking World of Ideas." *The Chronicle of Higher Education*. November 21, 2014.